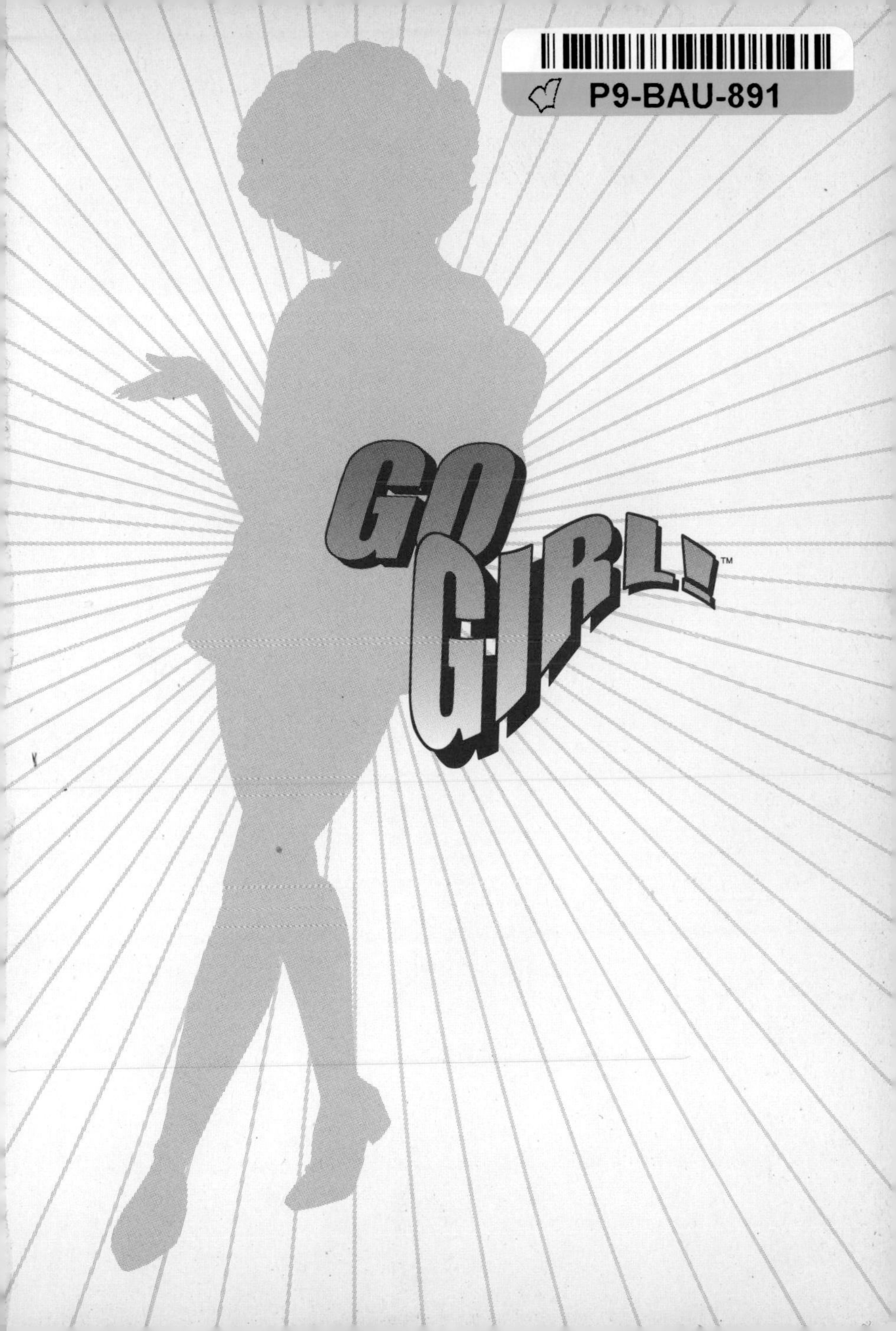
GO GIRL!™

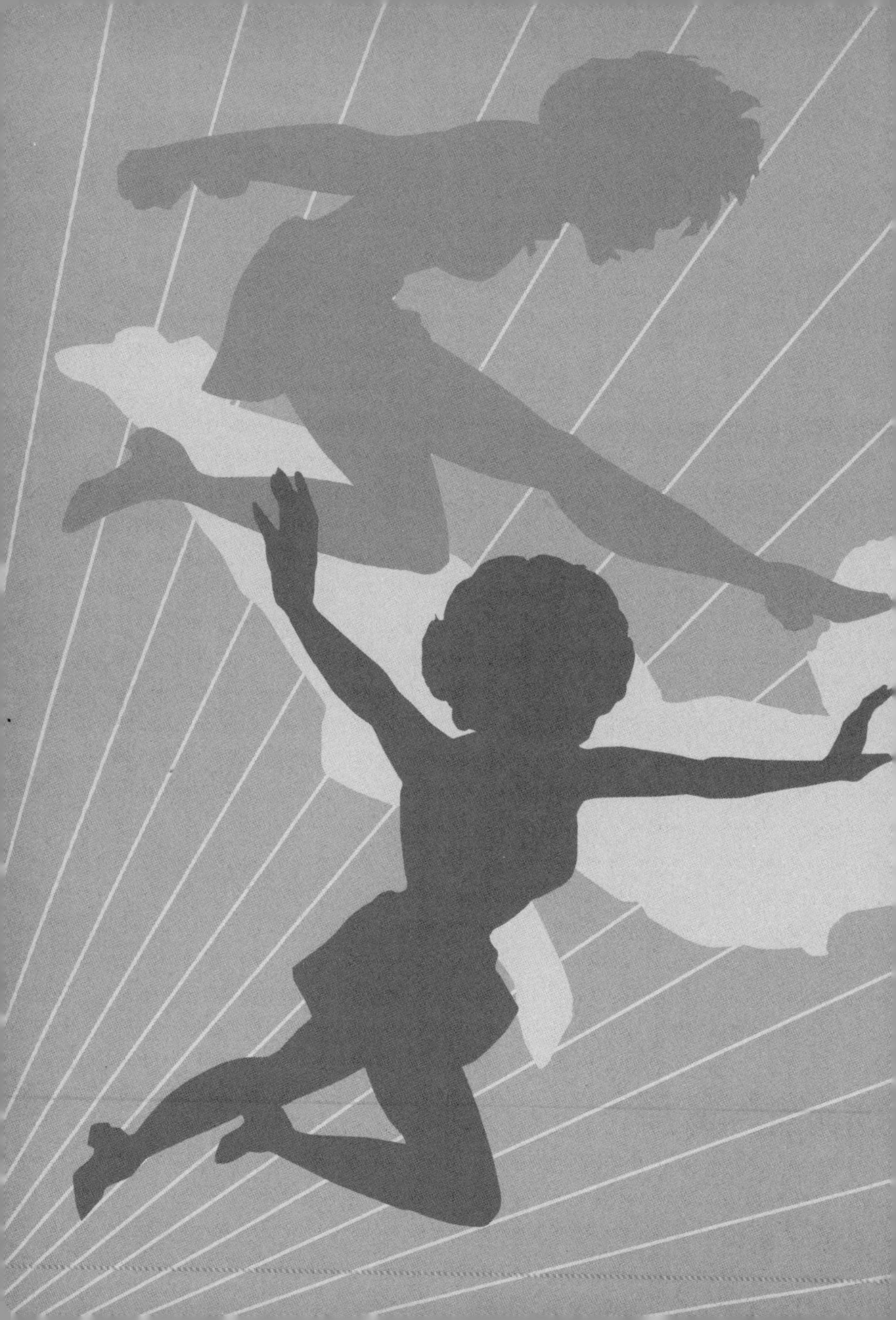

GO GIRL! 1

The Time Team

story **TRINA ROBBINS**

art **ANNE TIMMONS**

lettering **TRINA ROBBINS**

cover colors **CYNTHIA MARTIN**

DARK HORSE BOOKS™

publisher **MIKE RICHARDSON**

editor **CHRIS WARNER**

collection designer **DEBRA BAILEY**

art director **LIA RIBACCHI**

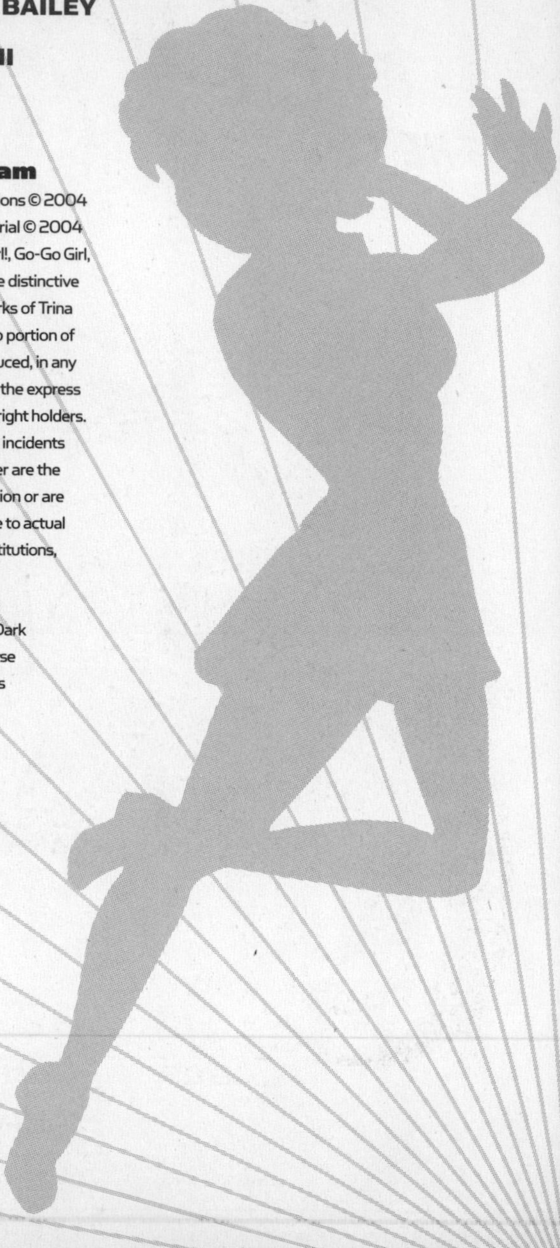

GOGIRL!™
Vol. 1: The Time Team

Published by
Dark Horse Books
A division of Dark Horse Comics, Inc.
10956 SE Main Street
Milwaukie, OR 97222

darkhorse.com

To find a comics shop in your area, call the Comic Shop Locator Service toll-free at 1-888-266-4226

First edition: September 2004
ISBN: 1-59307-230-9

10 9 8 7 6 5 4 3 2 1

PRINTED IN CANADA

GO GIRL!™

THE TIME TEAM

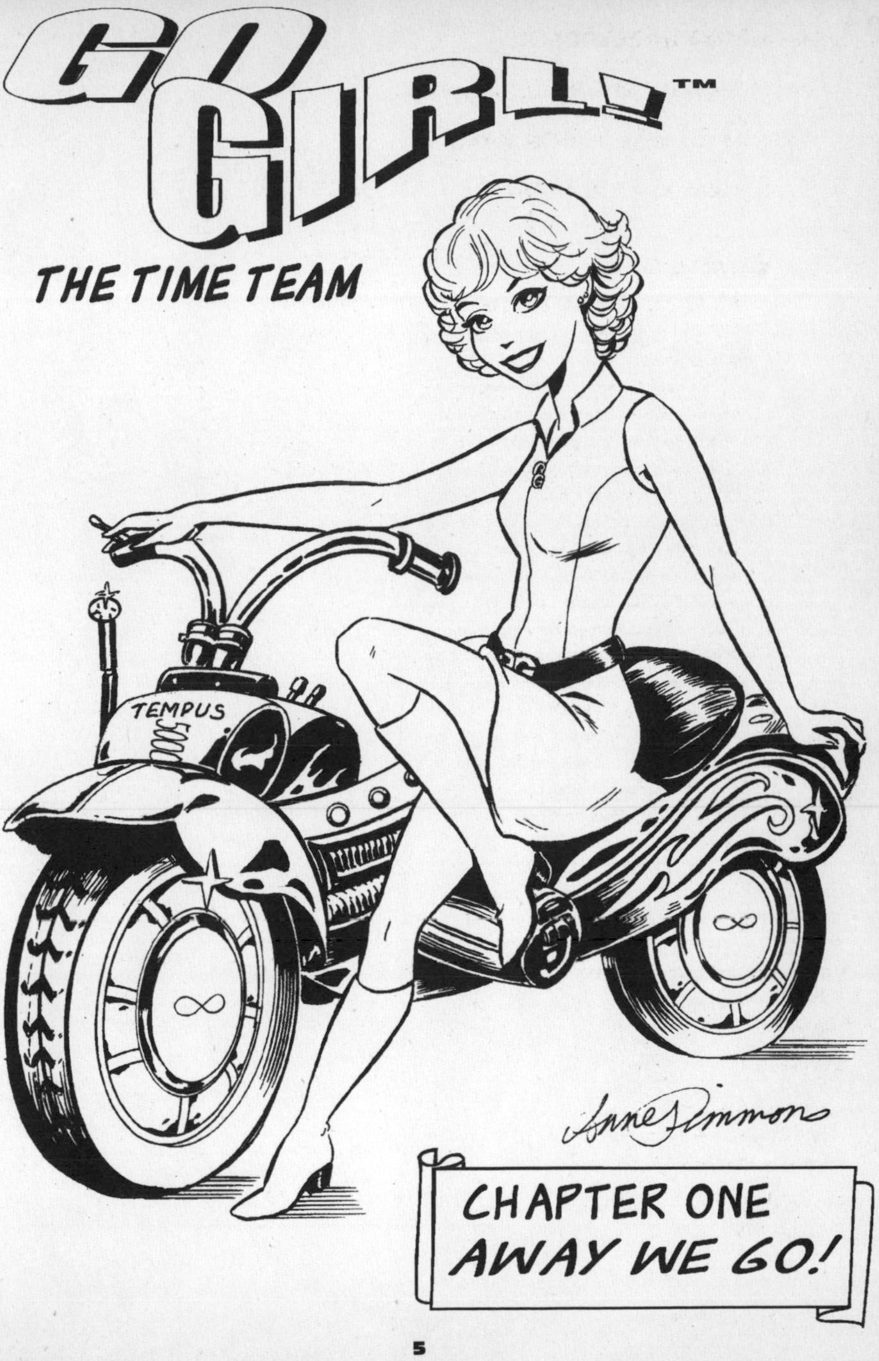
TEMPUS
5000
Anne Timmons

CHAPTER ONE
AWAY WE GO!

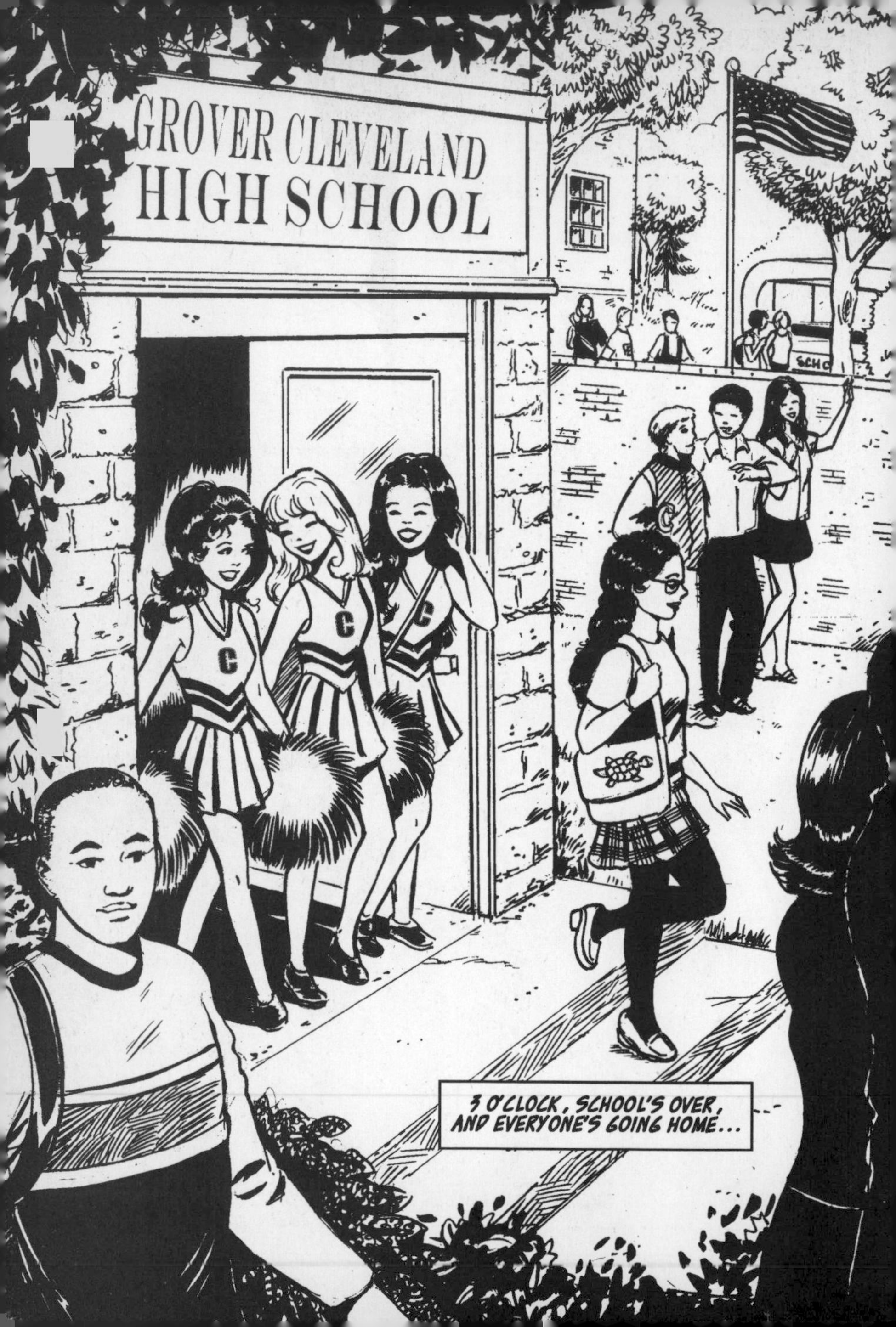
GROVER CLEVELAND HIGH SCHOOL
3 O'CLOCK, SCHOOL'S OVER, AND EVERYONE'S GOING HOME...

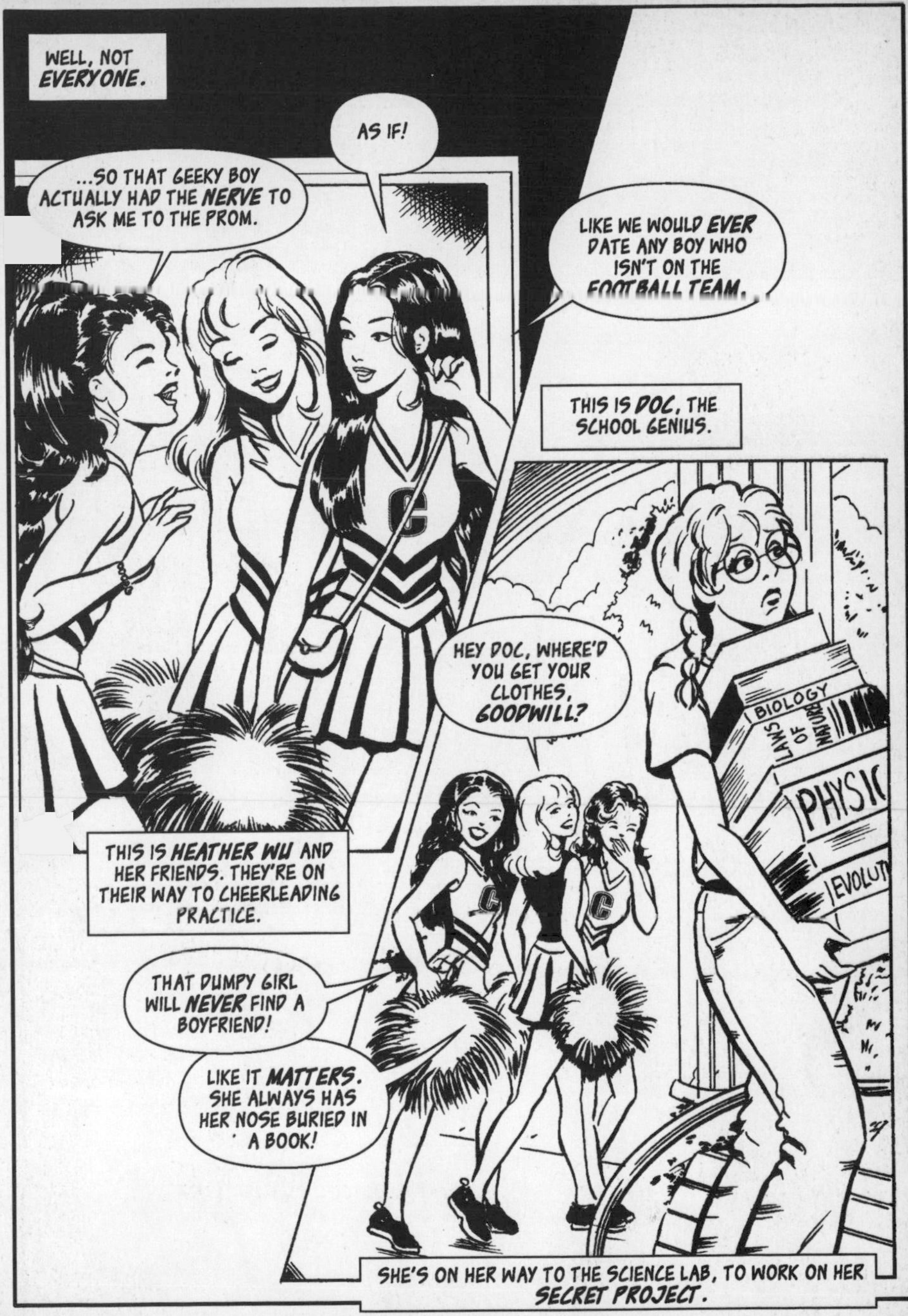

WELL, NOT EVERYONE.
...SO THAT GEEKY BOY ACTUALLY HAD THE NERVE TO ASK ME TO THE PROM.
AS IF!
LIKE WE WOULD EVER DATE ANY BOY WHO ISN'T ON THE FOOTBALL TEAM.
THIS IS HEATHER WU AND HER FRIENDS. THEY'RE ON THEIR WAY TO CHEERLEADING PRACTICE.
THIS IS DOC, THE SCHOOL GENIUS.
HEY DOC, WHERE'D YOU GET YOUR CLOTHES, GOODWILL?
BIOLOGY
LAWS OF NATURE
PHYSIC
EVOLUT
THAT DUMPY GIRL WILL NEVER FIND A BOYFRIEND!
LIKE IT MATTERS. SHE ALWAYS HAS HER NOSE BURIED IN A BOOK!
SHE'S ON HER WAY TO THE SCIENCE LAB, TO WORK ON HER SECRET PROJECT.

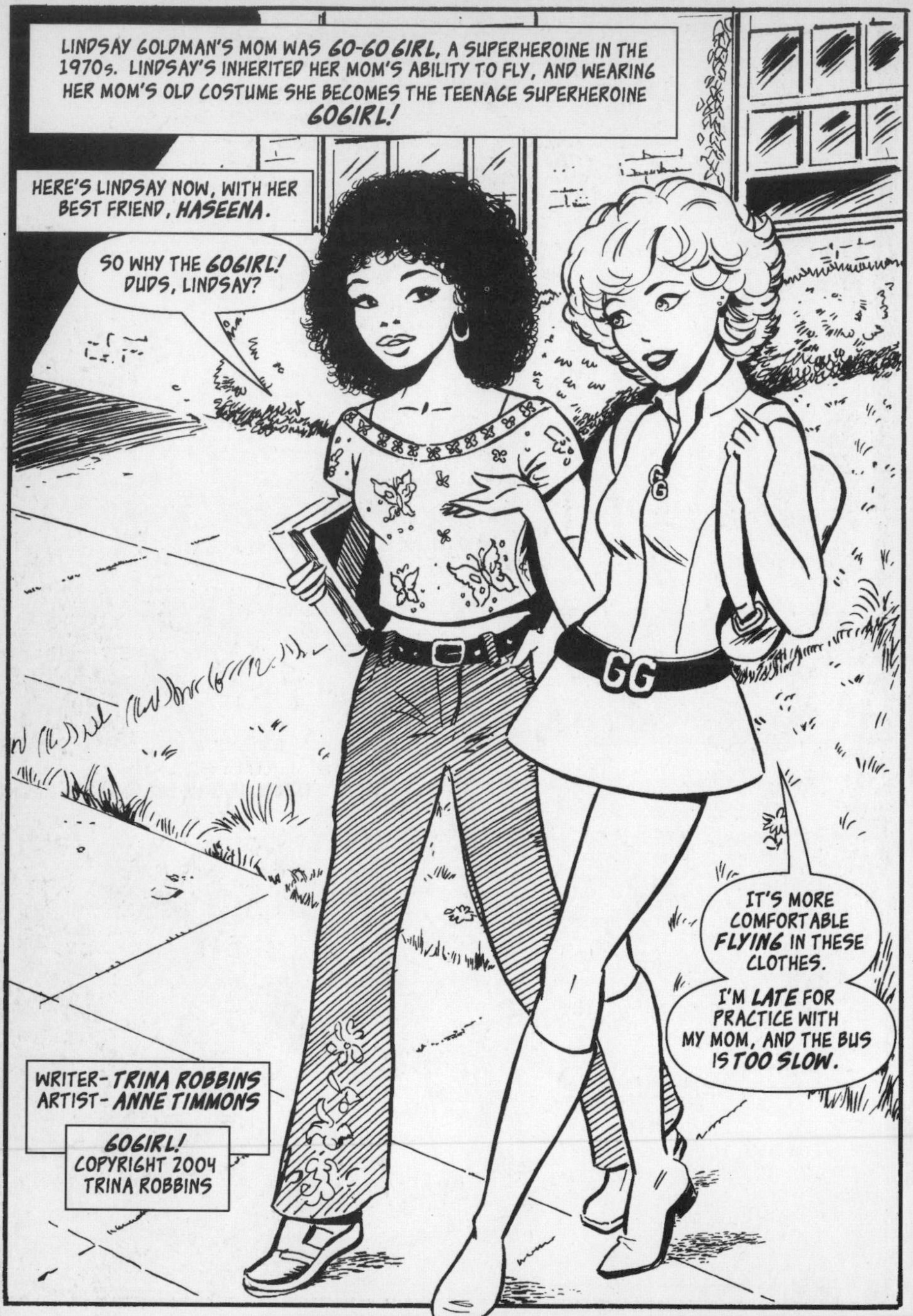
LINDSAY GOLDMAN'S MOM WAS GO-GO GIRL, A SUPERHEROINE IN THE 1970s. LINDSAY'S INHERITED HER MOM'S ABILITY TO FLY, AND WEARING HER MOM'S OLD COSTUME SHE BECOMES THE TEENAGE SUPERHEROINE GOGIRL!
HERE'S LINDSAY NOW, WITH HER BEST FRIEND, HASEENA.
SO WHY THE GOGIRL! DUDS, LINDSAY?
IT'S MORE COMFORTABLE FLYING IN THESE CLOTHES.
I'M LATE FOR PRACTICE WITH MY MOM, AND THE BUS IS TOO SLOW.
GG
WRITER- TRINA ROBBINS
ARTIST- ANNE TIMMONS
GOGIRL! COPYRIGHT 2004 TRINA ROBBINS

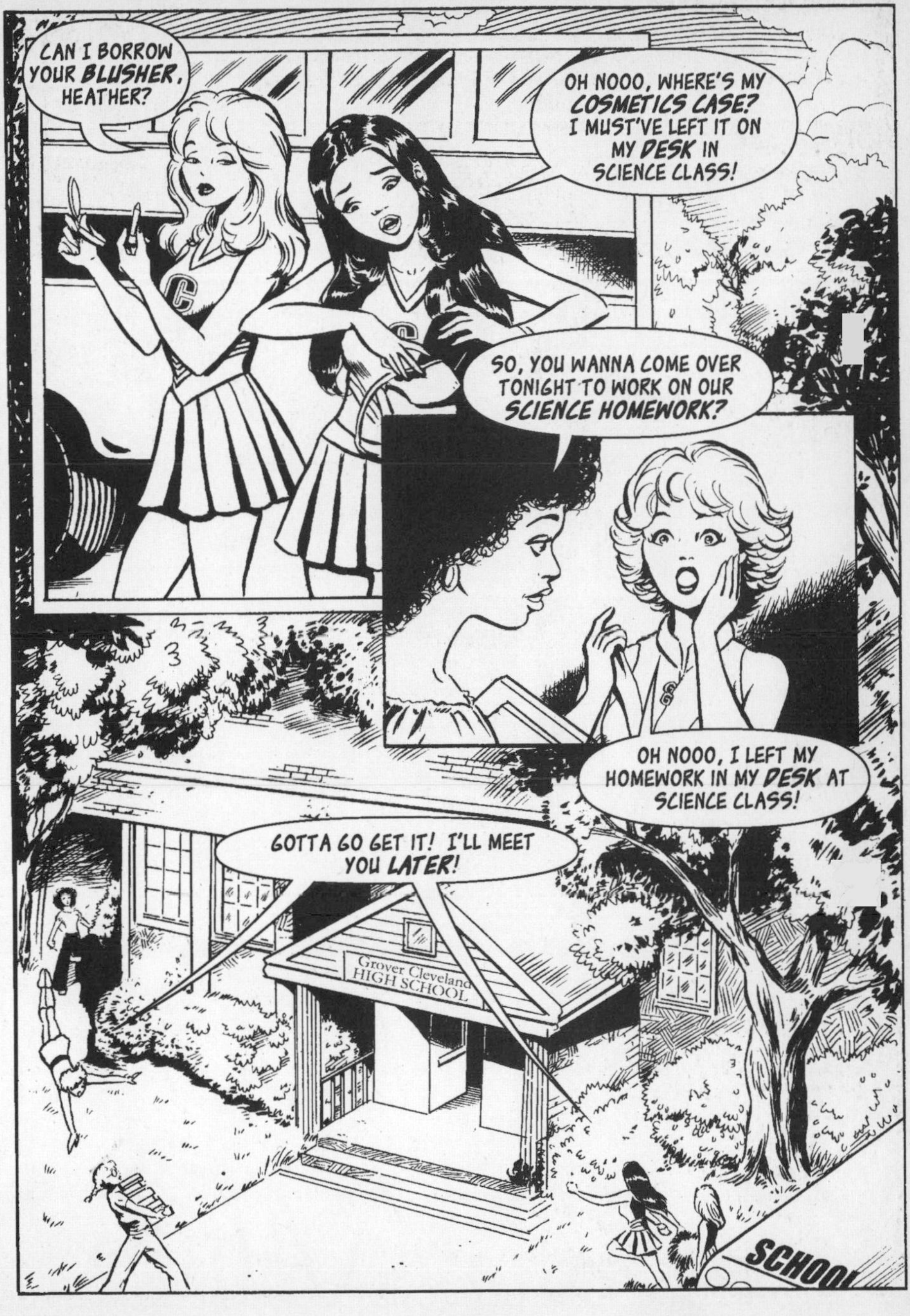
CAN I BORROW YOUR BLUSHER, HEATHER?
OH NOOO, WHERE'S MY COSMETICS CASE? I MUST'VE LEFT IT ON MY DESK IN SCIENCE CLASS!
SO, YOU WANNA COME OVER TONIGHT TO WORK ON OUR SCIENCE HOMEWORK?
OH NOOO, I LEFT MY HOMEWORK IN MY DESK AT SCIENCE CLASS!
GOTTA GO GET IT! I'LL MEET YOU LATER!
Grover Cleveland HIGH SCHOOL
SCHOO

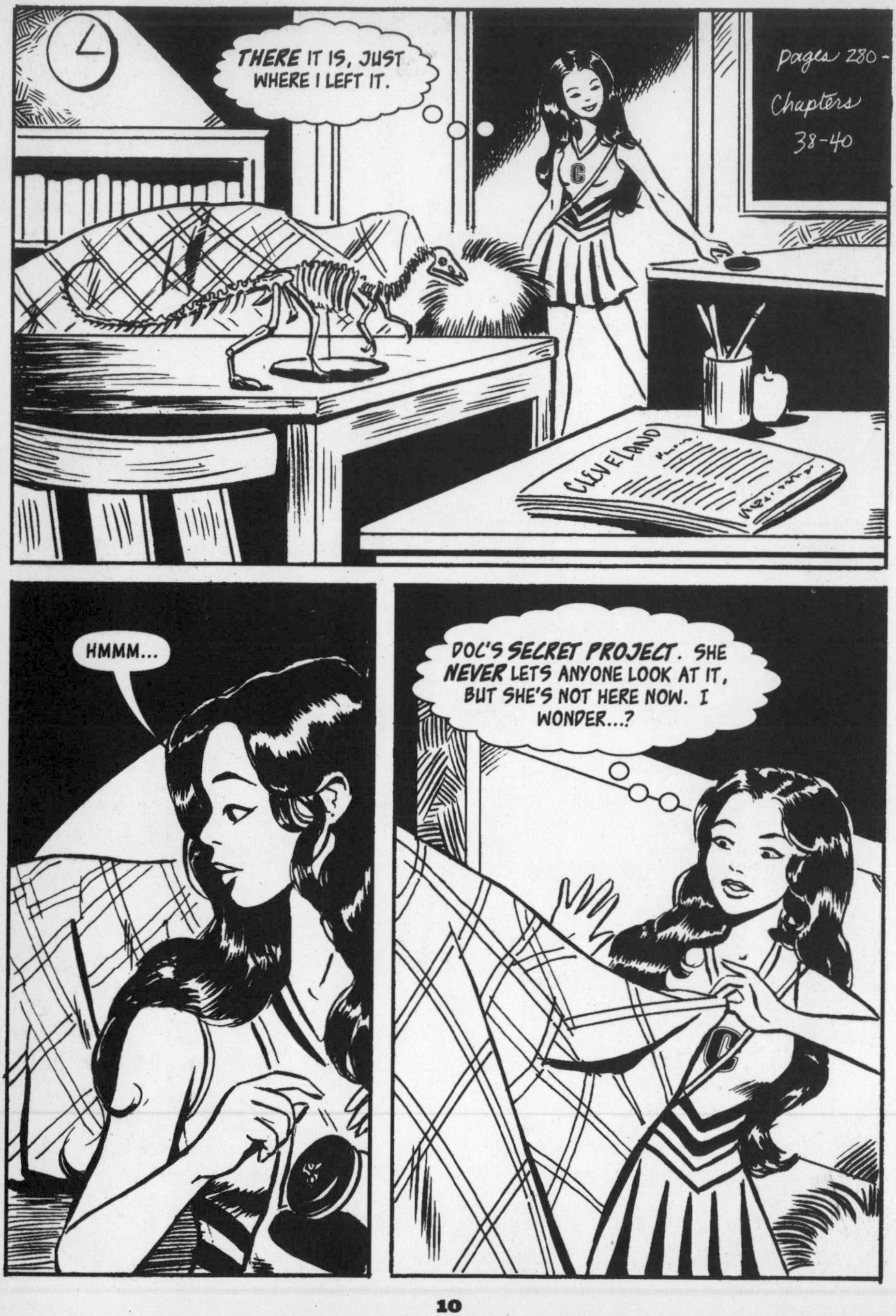
THERE IT IS, JUST WHERE I LEFT IT.
Pages 280-
Chapters 38-40
CLEVELAND
HMMM...
DOC'S SECRET PROJECT. SHE NEVER LETS ANYONE LOOK AT IT, BUT SHE'S NOT HERE NOW. I WONDER...?

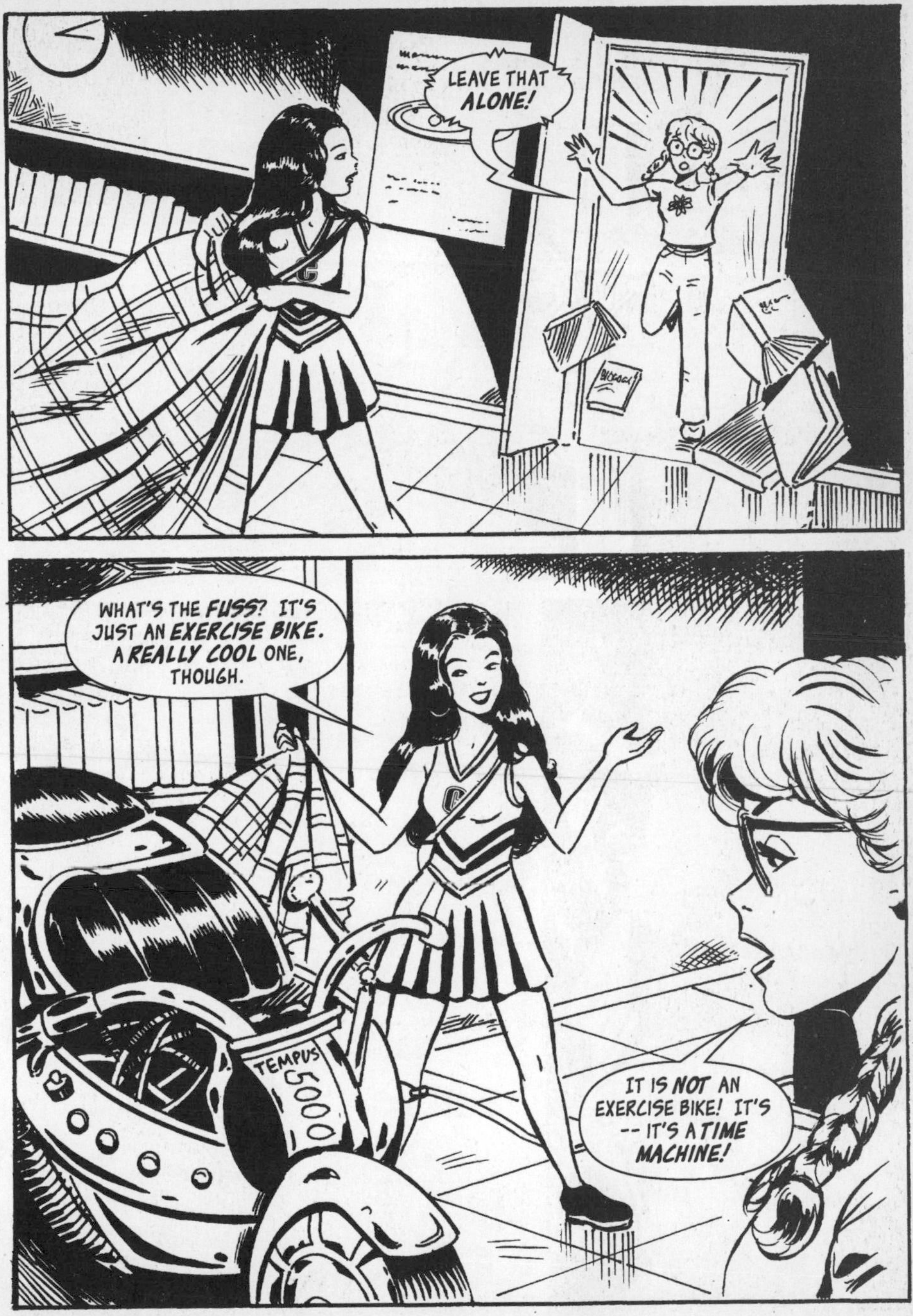
LEAVE THAT ALONE!
WHAT'S THE FUSS? IT'S JUST AN EXERCISE BIKE. A REALLY COOL ONE, THOUGH.
TEMPUS 5000
IT IS NOT AN EXERCISE BIKE! IT'S -- IT'S A TIME MACHINE!

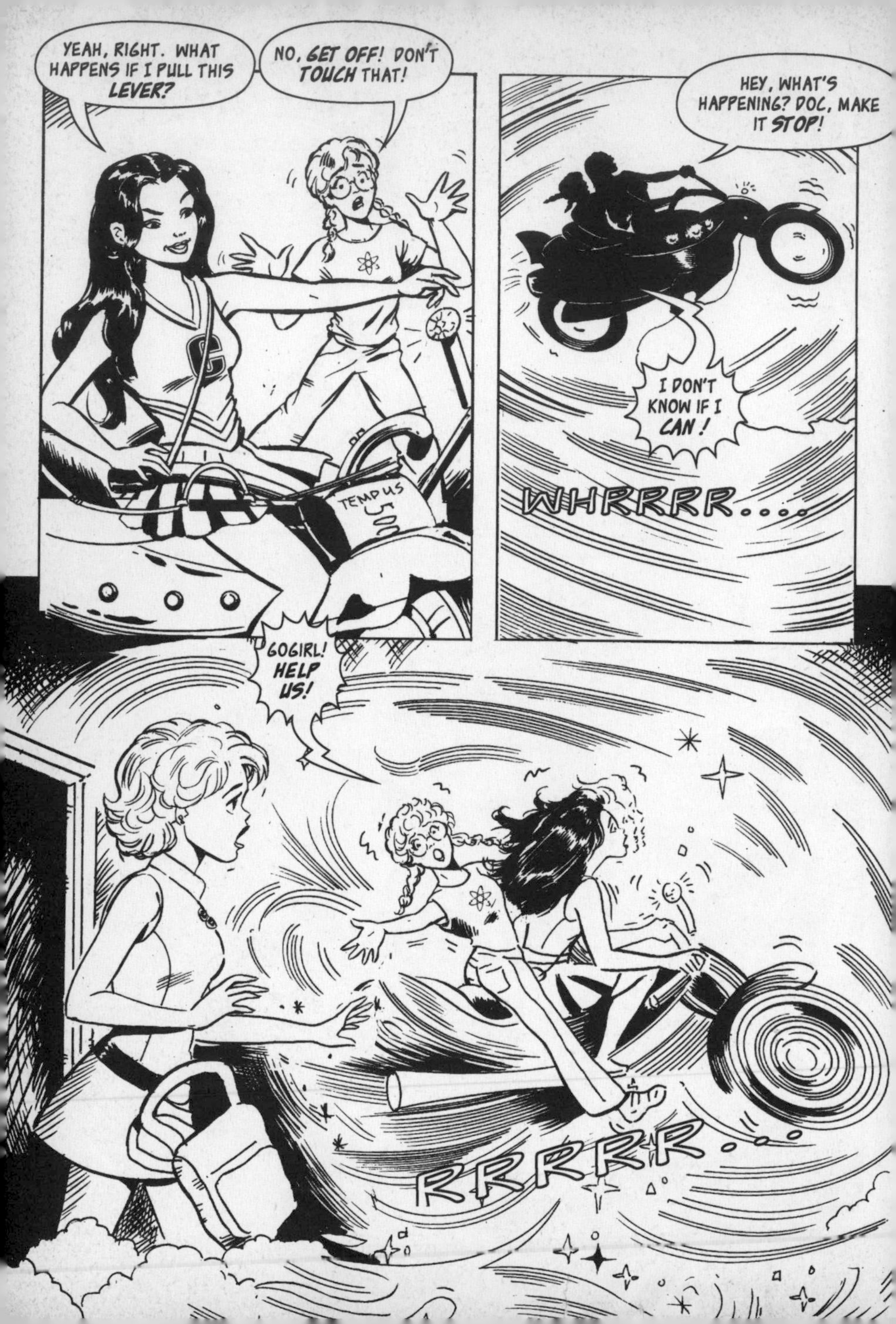
YEAH, RIGHT. WHAT HAPPENS IF I PULL THIS LEVER?
NO, GET OFF! DON'T TOUCH THAT!
TEMPUS 500
HEY, WHAT'S HAPPENING? DOC, MAKE IT STOP!
I DON'T KNOW IF I CAN!
WHRRRRR.....
GOGIRL! HELP US!
RRRRRR...

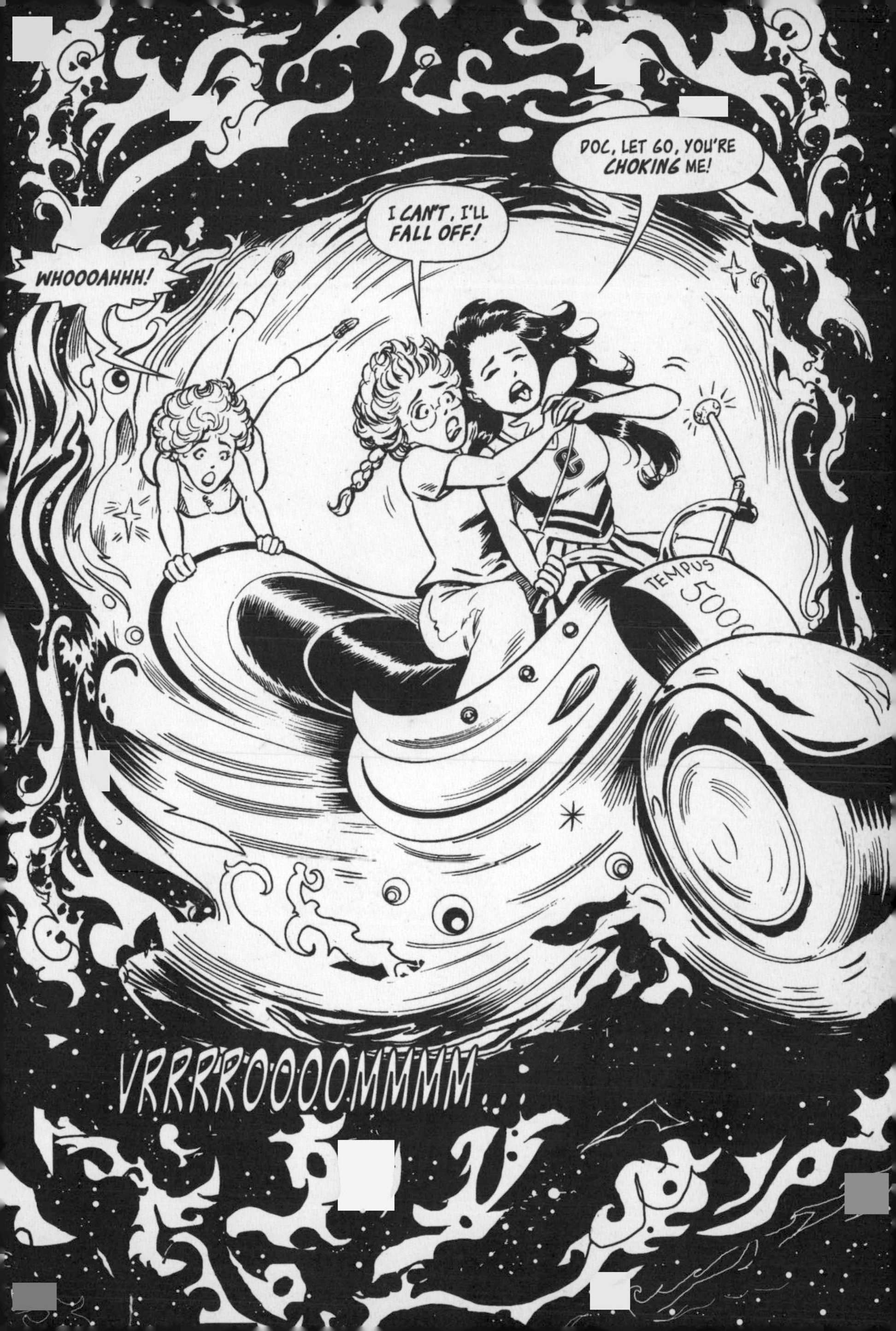
WHOOOAHHH!
DOC, LET GO, YOU'RE CHOKING ME!
I CAN'T, I'LL FALL OFF!
TEMPUS
VRRRROOOOMMMMM...

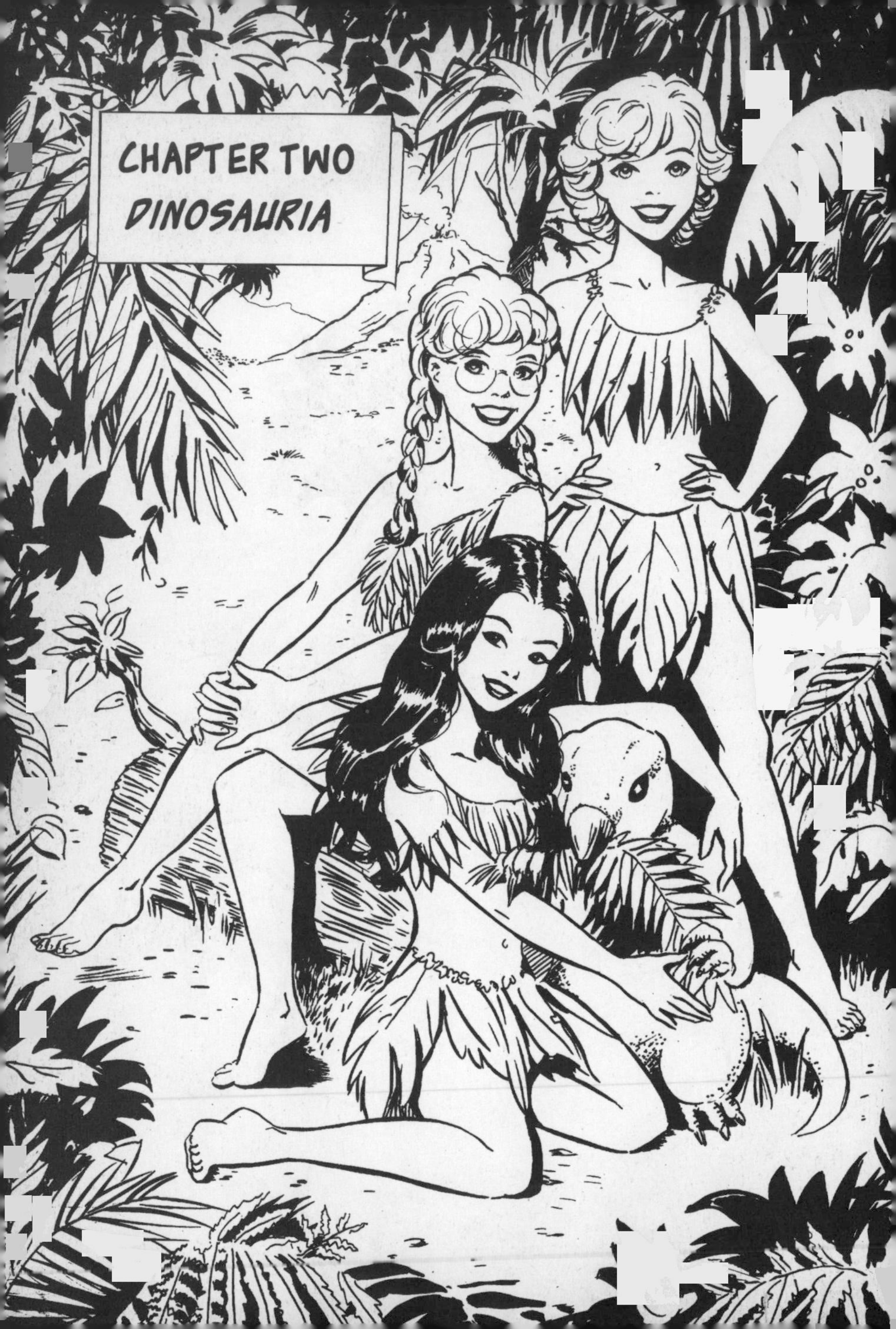
CHAPTER TWO
DINOSAURIA

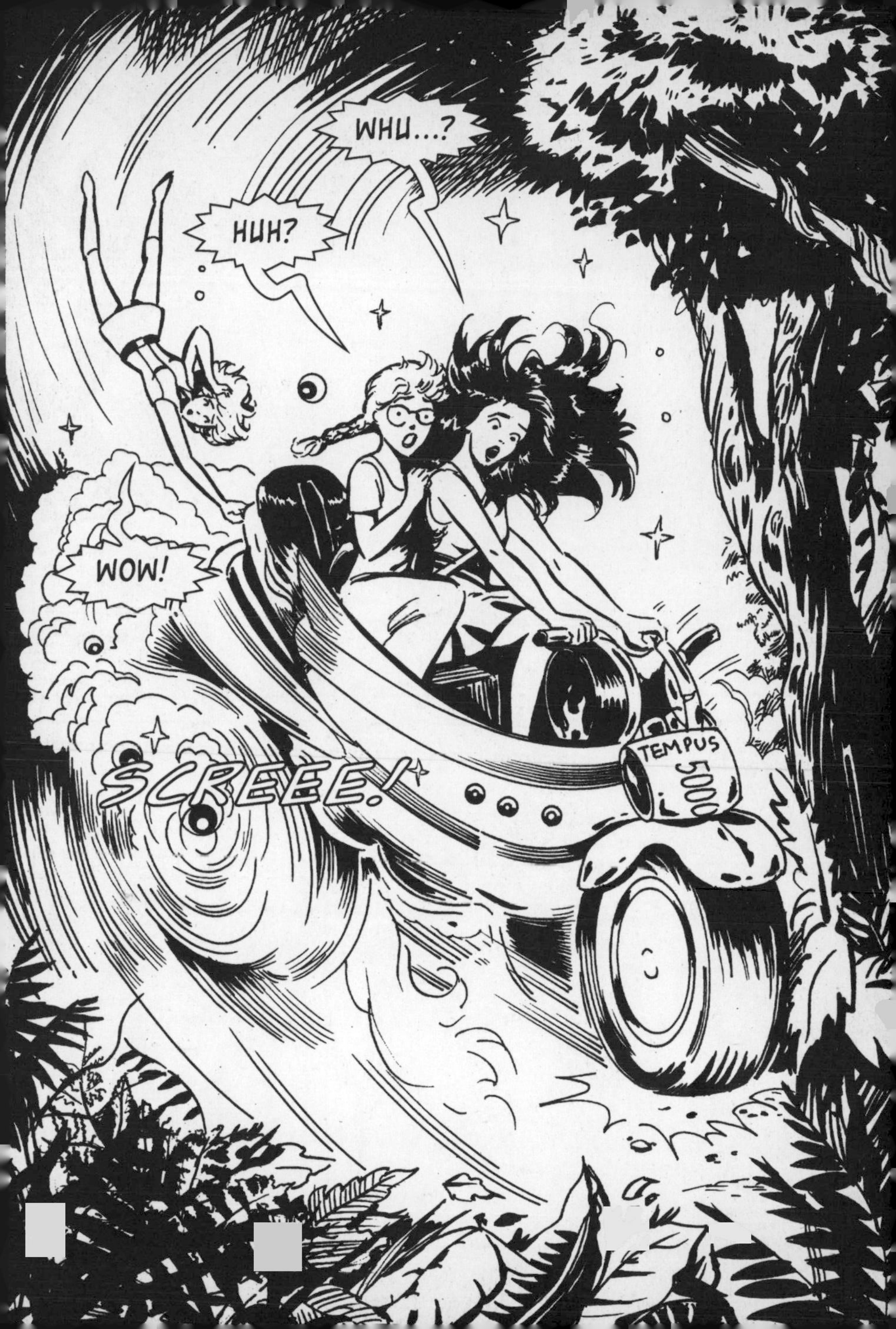
WHU...?
HUH?
WOW!
SCREEE!
TEMPUS 5000

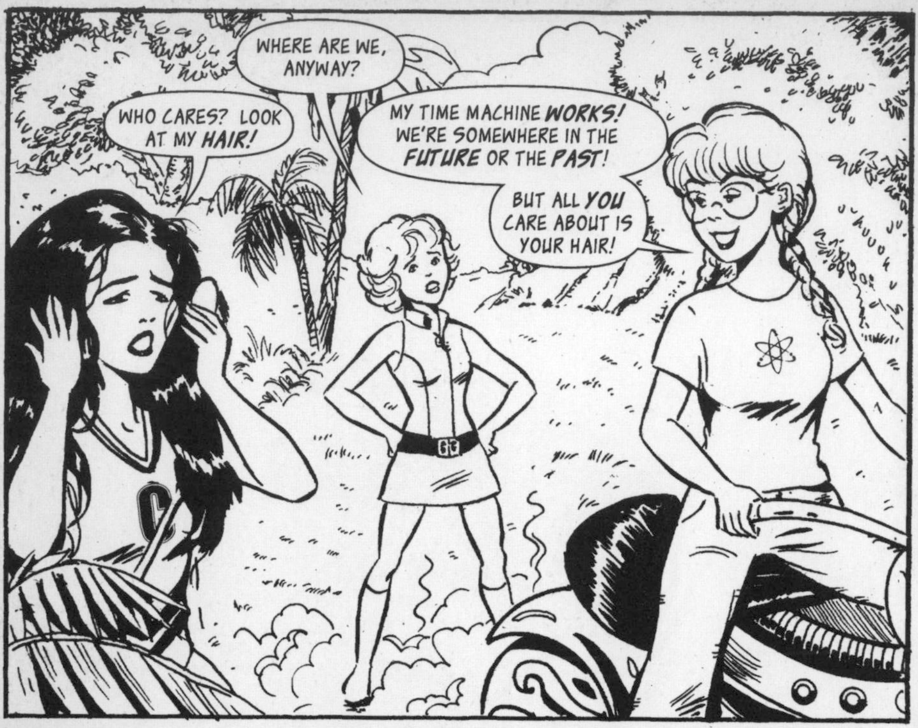
WHERE ARE WE, ANYWAY?
WHO CARES? LOOK AT MY HAIR!
MY TIME MACHINE WORKS! WE'RE SOMEWHERE IN THE FUTURE OR THE PAST!
BUT ALL YOU CARE ABOUT IS YOUR HAIR!

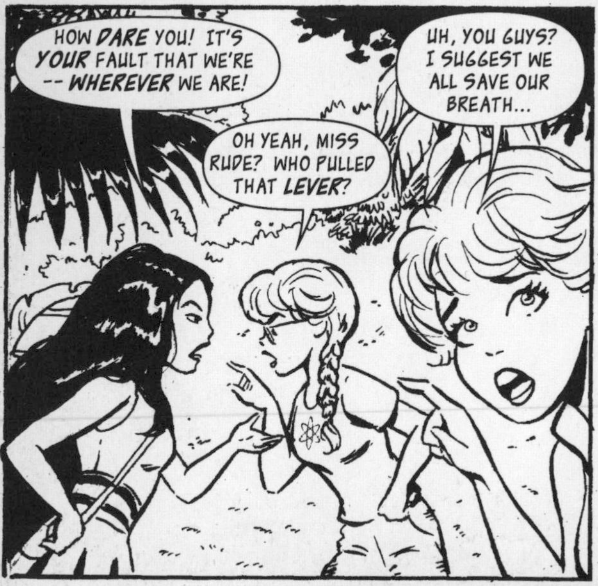
HOW DARE YOU! IT'S YOUR FAULT THAT WE'RE -- WHEREVER WE ARE!
OH YEAH, MISS RUDE? WHO PULLED THAT LEVER?
UH, YOU GUYS? I SUGGEST WE ALL SAVE OUR BREATH...

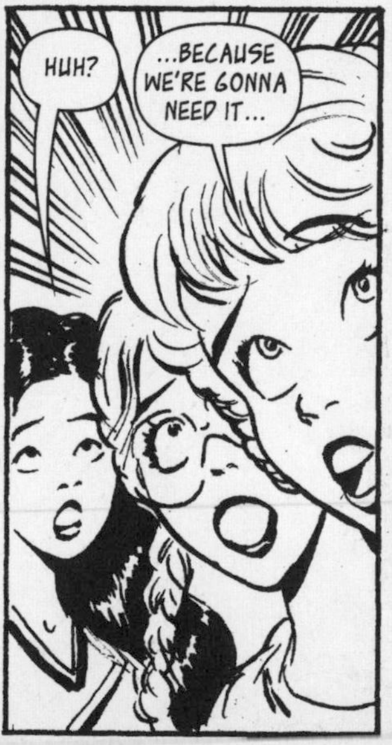
HUH?
...BECAUSE WE'RE GONNA NEED IT...

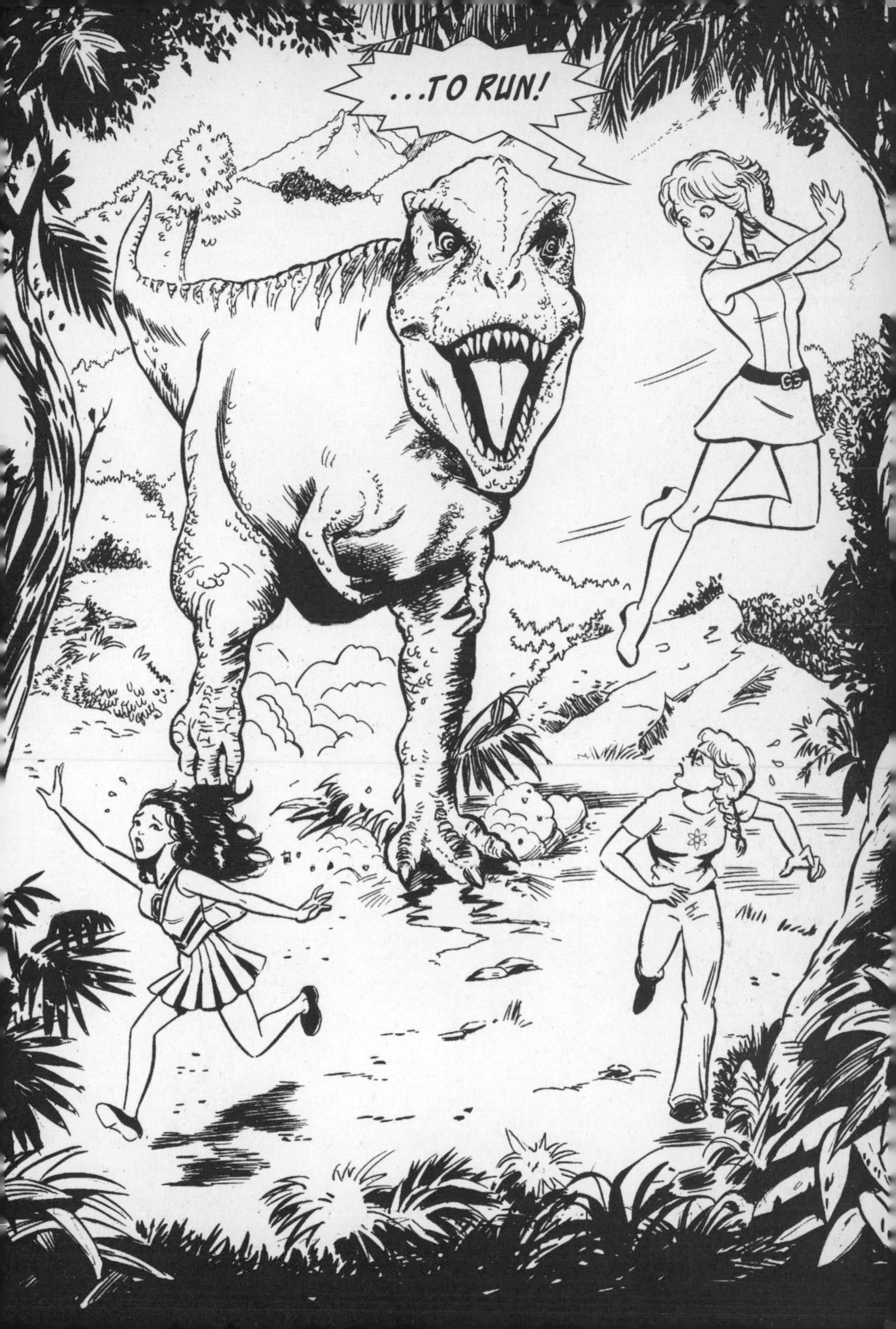
...TO RUN!

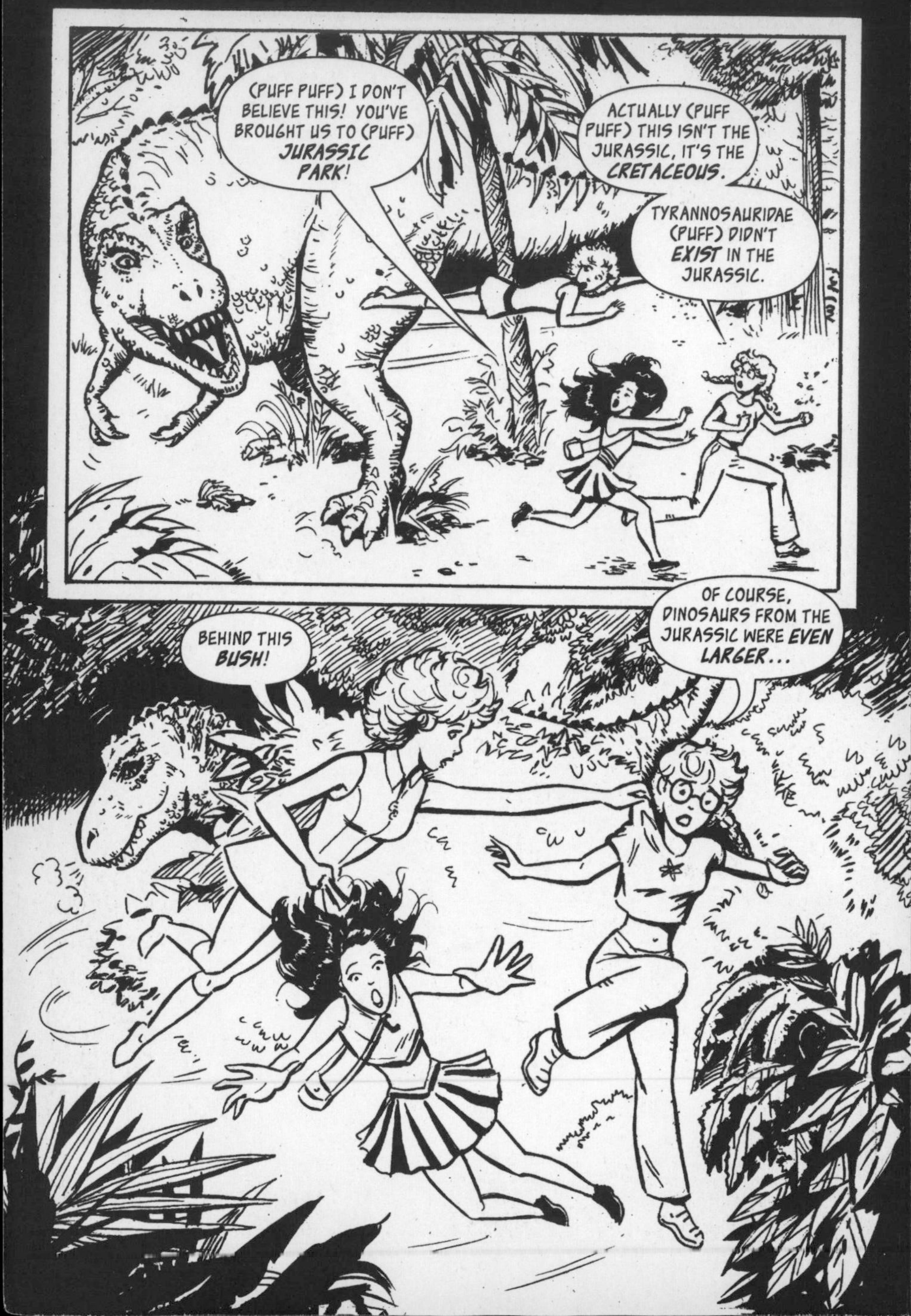
(PUFF PUFF) I DON'T BELIEVE THIS! YOU'VE BROUGHT US TO (PUFF) JURASSIC PARK!
ACTUALLY (PUFF PUFF) THIS ISN'T THE JURASSIC, IT'S THE CRETACEOUS.
TYRANNOSAURIDAE (PUFF) DIDN'T EXIST IN THE JURASSIC.
BEHIND THIS BUSH!
OF COURSE, DINOSAURS FROM THE JURASSIC WERE EVEN LARGER...

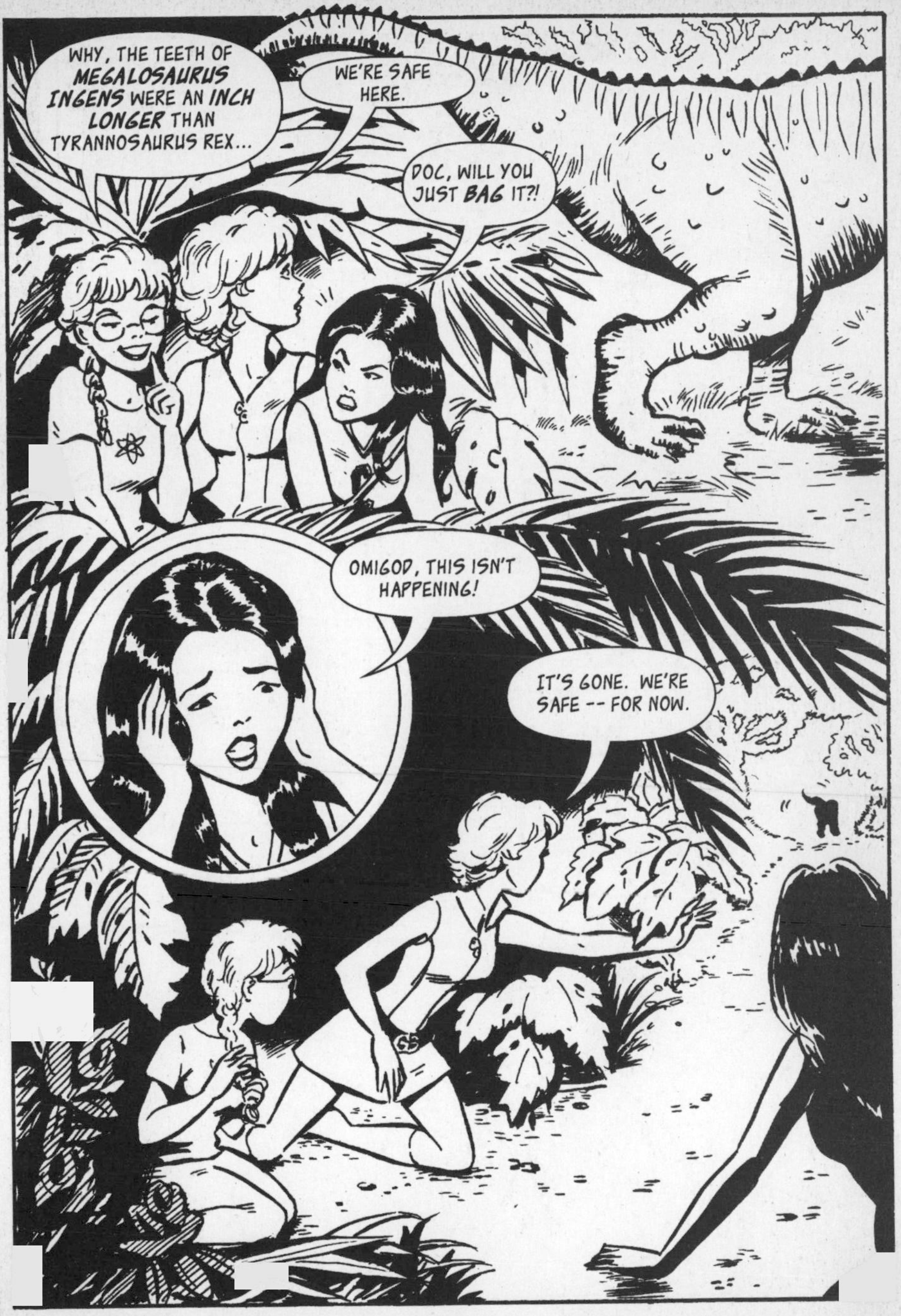
WHY, THE TEETH OF MEGALOSAURUS INGENS WERE AN INCH LONGER THAN TYRANNOSAURUS REX...
WE'RE SAFE HERE.
DOC, WILL YOU JUST BAG IT?!
OMIGOD, THIS ISN'T HAPPENING!
IT'S GONE. WE'RE SAFE -- FOR NOW.

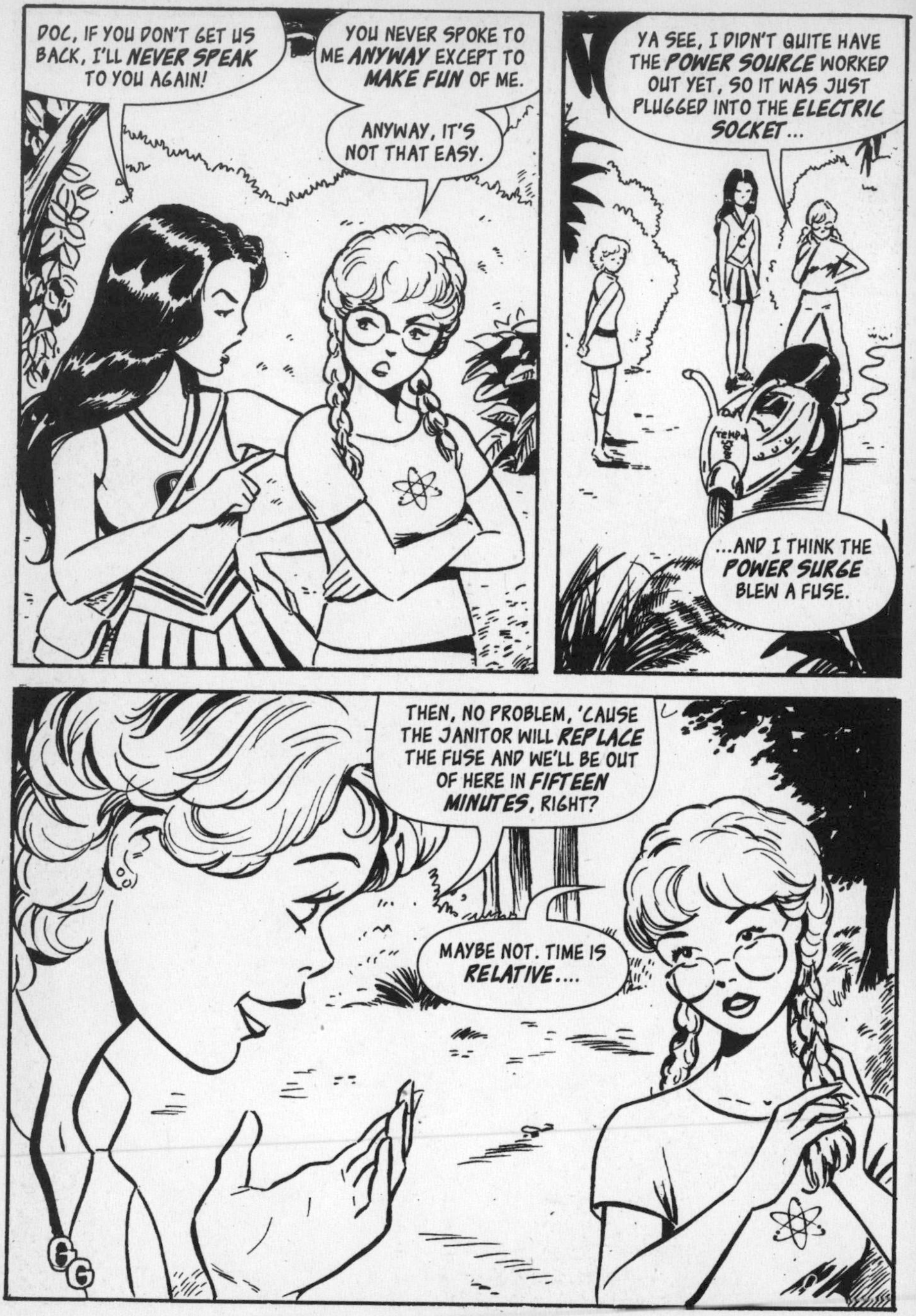
DOC, IF YOU DON'T GET US BACK, I'LL NEVER SPEAK TO YOU AGAIN!
YOU NEVER SPOKE TO ME ANYWAY EXCEPT TO MAKE FUN OF ME.
ANYWAY, IT'S NOT THAT EASY.
YA SEE, I DIDN'T QUITE HAVE THE POWER SOURCE WORKED OUT YET, SO IT WAS JUST PLUGGED INTO THE ELECTRIC SOCKET...
...AND I THINK THE POWER SURGE BLEW A FUSE.
THEN, NO PROBLEM, 'CAUSE THE JANITOR WILL REPLACE THE FUSE AND WE'LL BE OUT OF HERE IN FIFTEEN MINUTES, RIGHT?
MAYBE NOT. TIME IS RELATIVE....

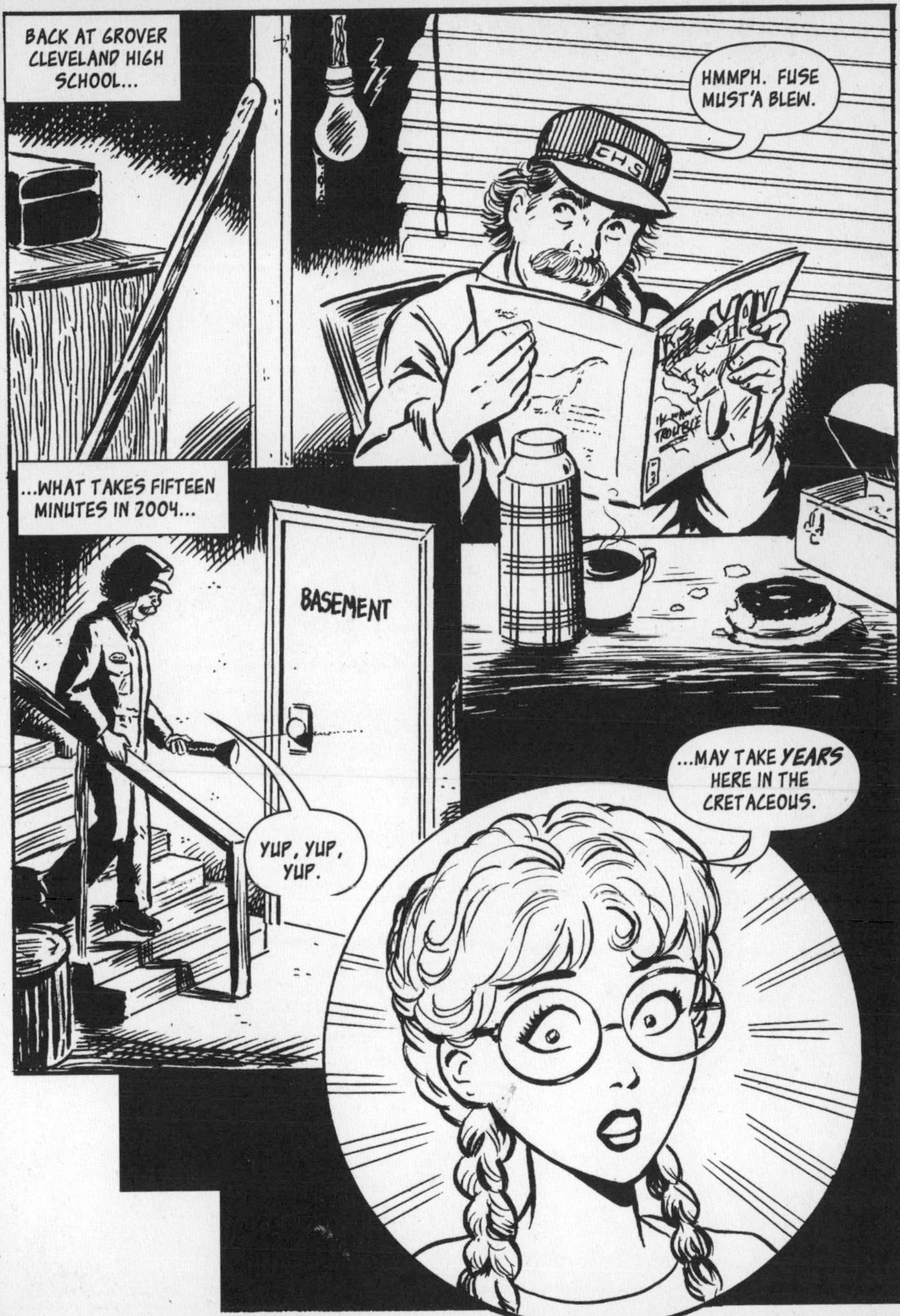
BACK AT GROVER CLEVELAND HIGH SCHOOL...
HMMPH. FUSE MUST'A BLEW.
...WHAT TAKES FIFTEEN MINUTES IN 2004...
BASEMENT
YUP, YUP, YUP.
...MAY TAKE YEARS HERE IN THE CRETACEOUS.

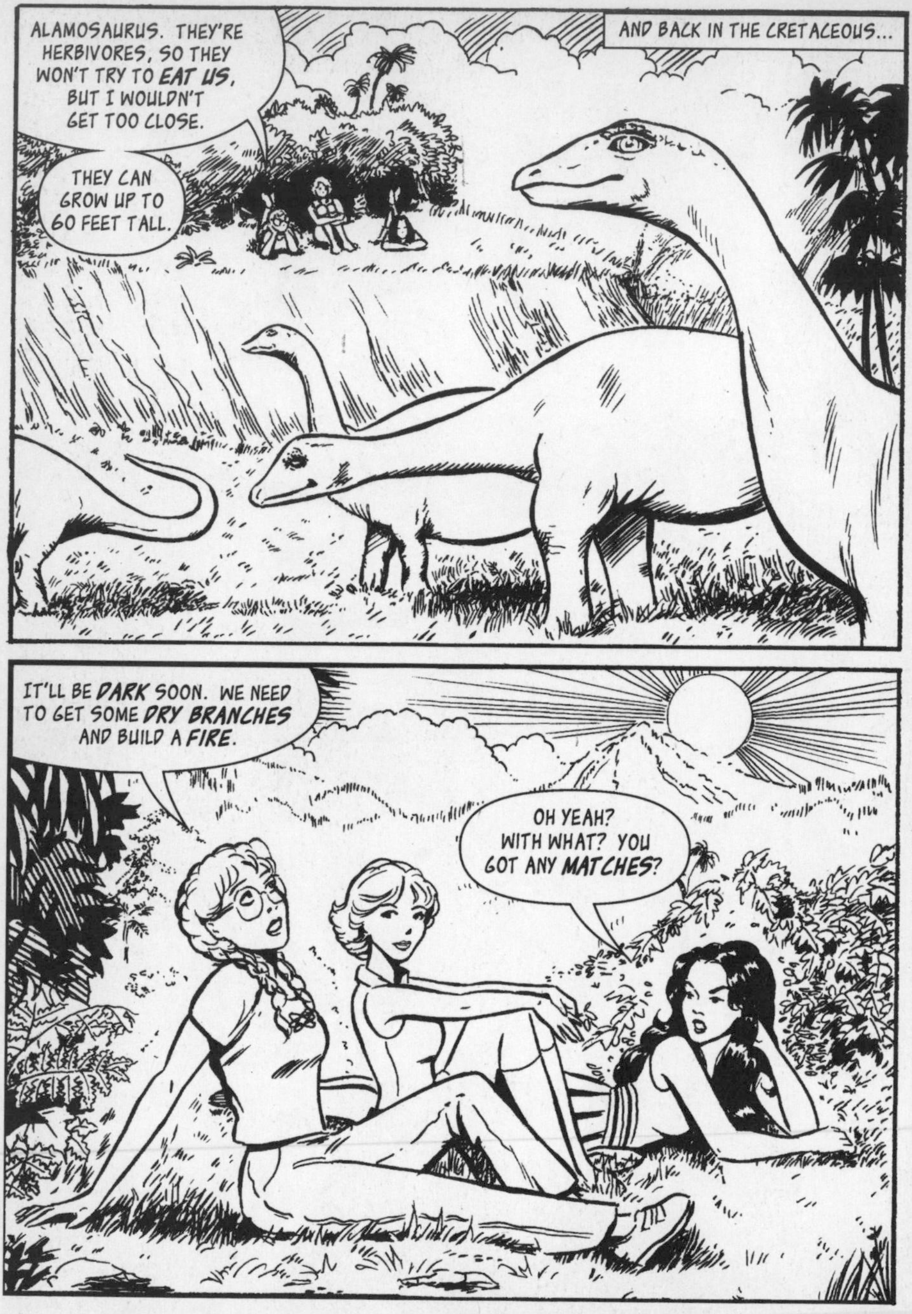
AND BACK IN THE CRETACEOUS...
ALAMOSAURUS. THEY'RE HERBIVORES, SO THEY WON'T TRY TO EAT US, BUT I WOULDN'T GET TOO CLOSE.
THEY CAN GROW UP TO 60 FEET TALL.
IT'LL BE DARK SOON. WE NEED TO GET SOME DRY BRANCHES AND BUILD A FIRE.
OH YEAH? WITH WHAT? YOU GOT ANY MATCHES?

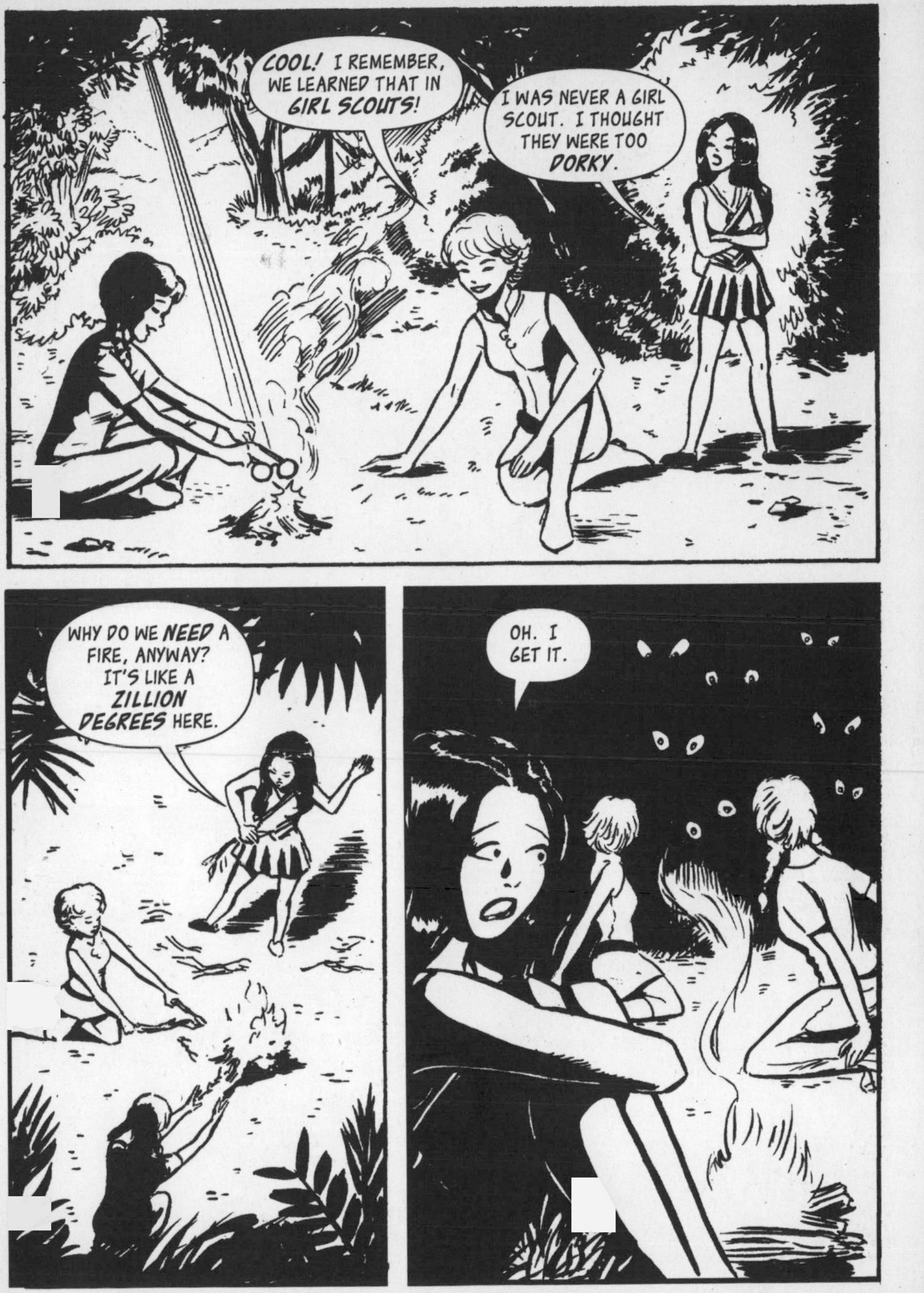
COOL! I REMEMBER, WE LEARNED THAT IN GIRL SCOUTS!
I WAS NEVER A GIRL SCOUT. I THOUGHT THEY WERE TOO DORKY.
WHY DO WE NEED A FIRE, ANYWAY? IT'S LIKE A ZILLION DEGREES HERE.
OH. I GET IT.

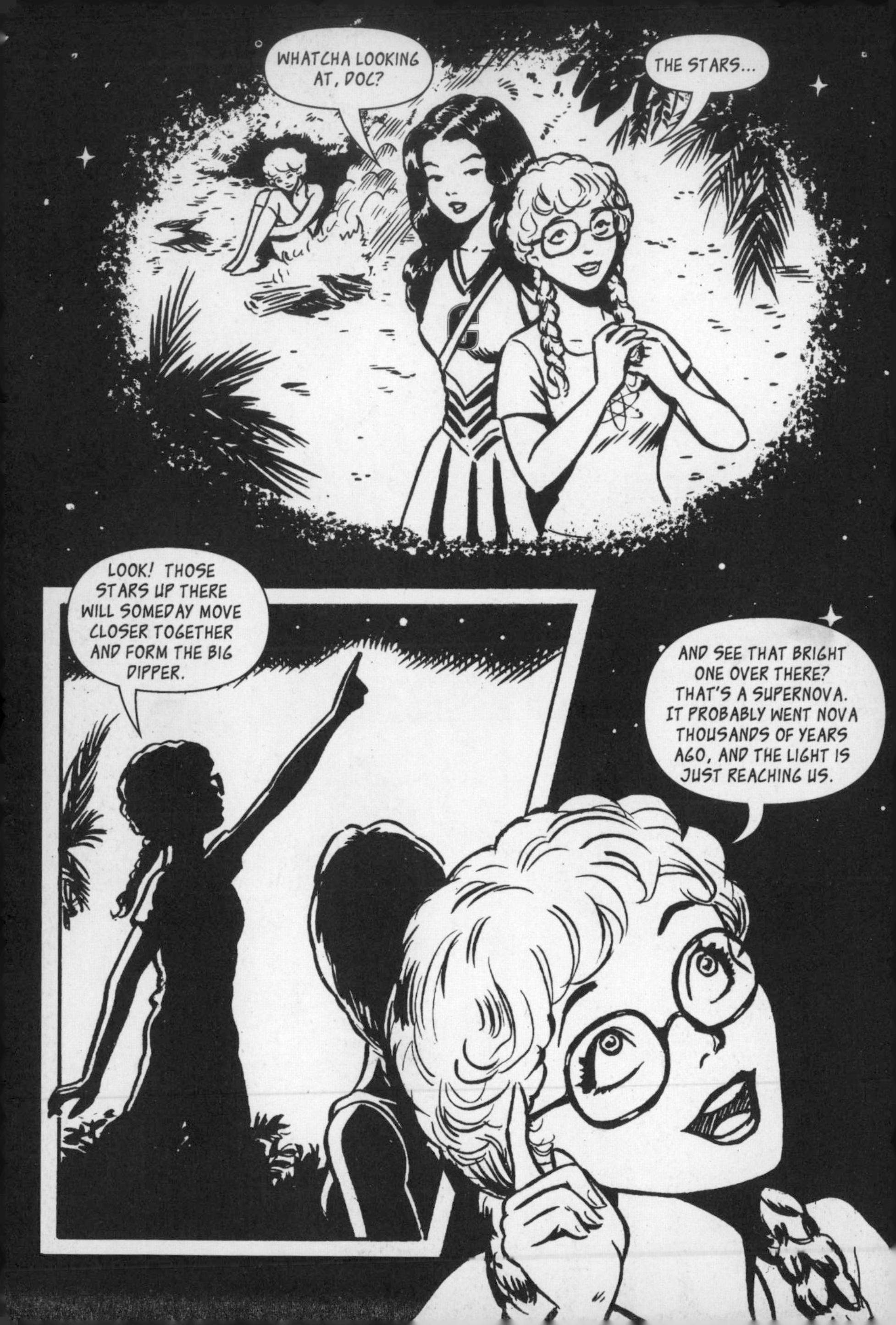
WHATCHA LOOKING AT, DOC?
THE STARS...
LOOK! THOSE STARS UP THERE WILL SOMEDAY MOVE CLOSER TOGETHER AND FORM THE BIG DIPPER.
AND SEE THAT BRIGHT ONE OVER THERE? THAT'S A SUPERNOVA. IT PROBABLY WENT NOVA THOUSANDS OF YEARS AGO, AND THE LIGHT IS JUST REACHING US.

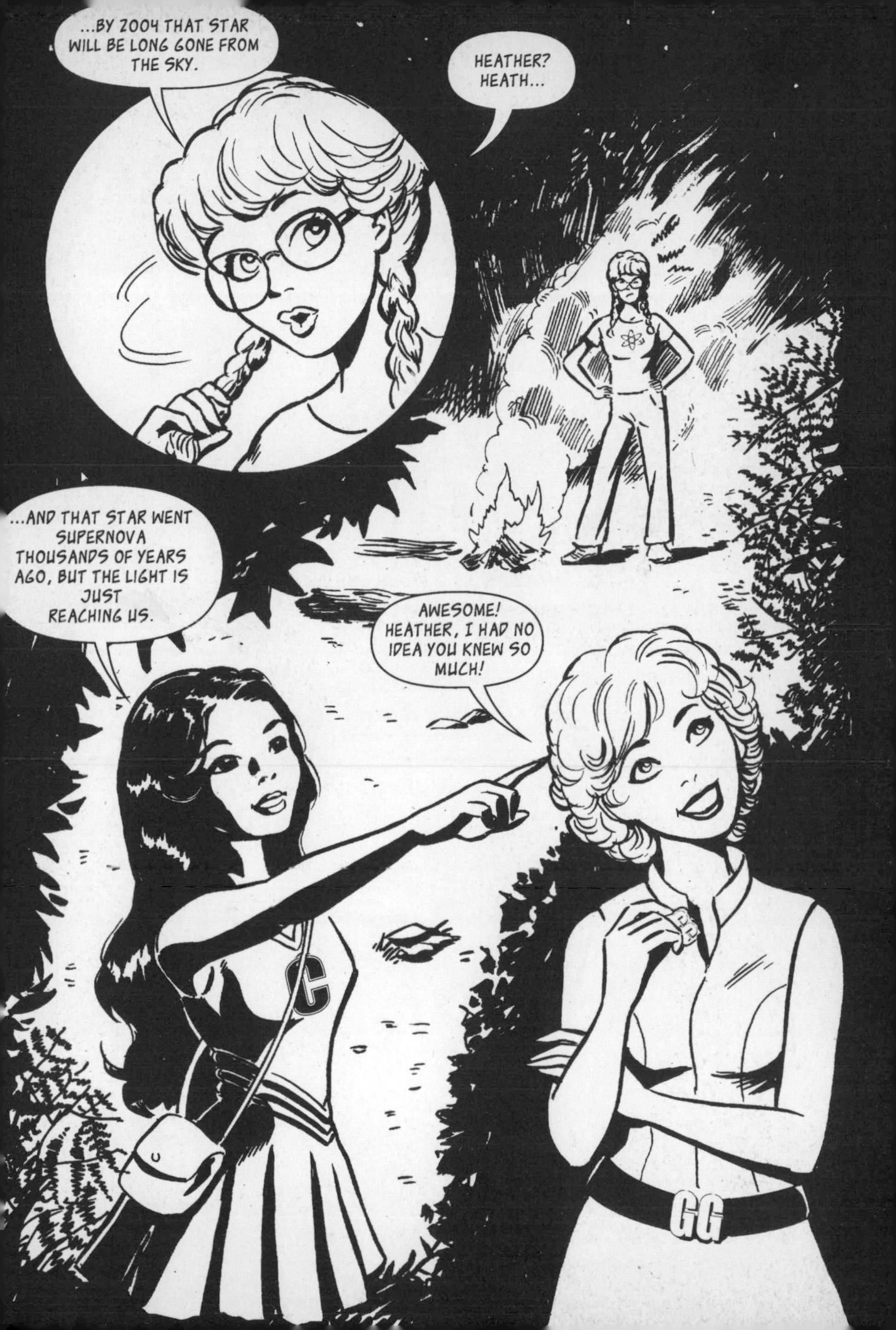
...BY 2004 THAT STAR WILL BE LONG GONE FROM THE SKY.
HEATHER? HEATH...
...AND THAT STAR WENT SUPERNOVA THOUSANDS OF YEARS AGO, BUT THE LIGHT IS JUST REACHING US.
AWESOME! HEATHER, I HAD NO IDEA YOU KNEW SO MUCH!

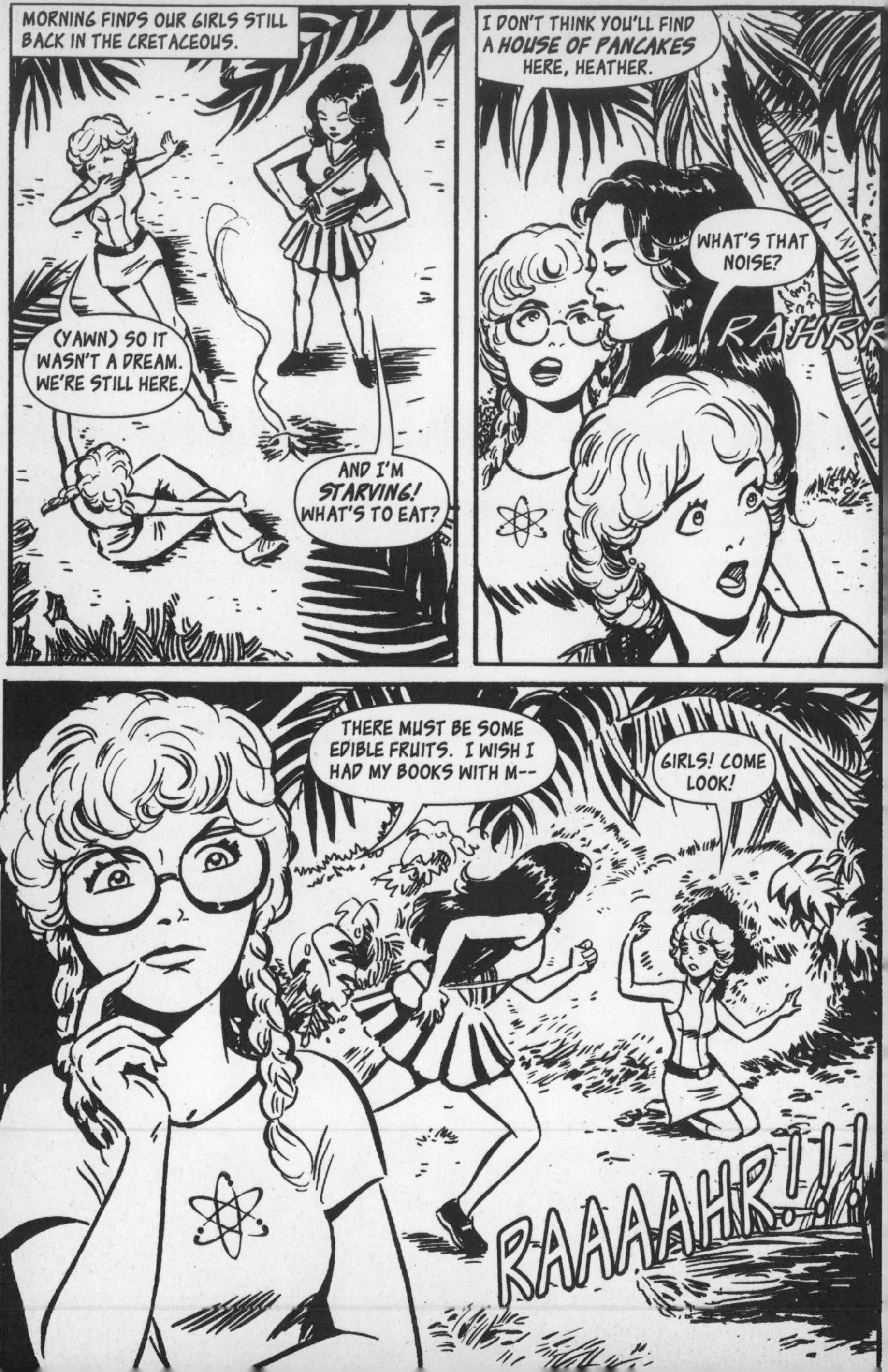
MORNING FINDS OUR GIRLS STILL BACK IN THE CRETACEOUS.
(YAWN) SO IT WASN'T A DREAM. WE'RE STILL HERE.
AND I'M STARVING! WHAT'S TO EAT?
I DON'T THINK YOU'LL FIND A HOUSE OF PANCAKES HERE, HEATHER.
WHAT'S THAT NOISE?
RAHRR
THERE MUST BE SOME EDIBLE FRUITS. I WISH I HAD MY BOOKS WITH M--
GIRLS! COME LOOK!
RAAAAHR!!!

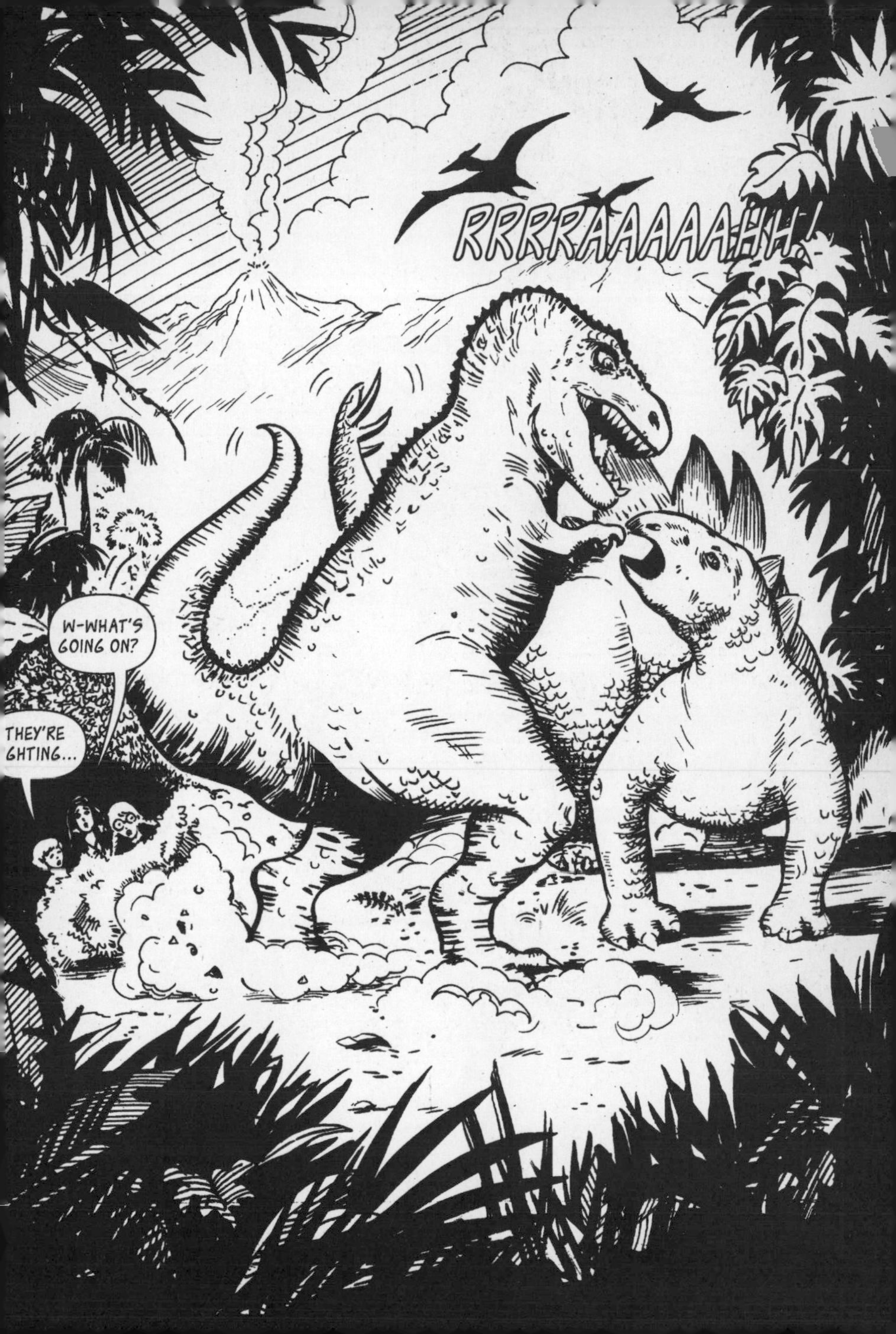
RRRRAAAAAAHH!
W-WHAT'S GOING ON?
THEY'RE GHTING...

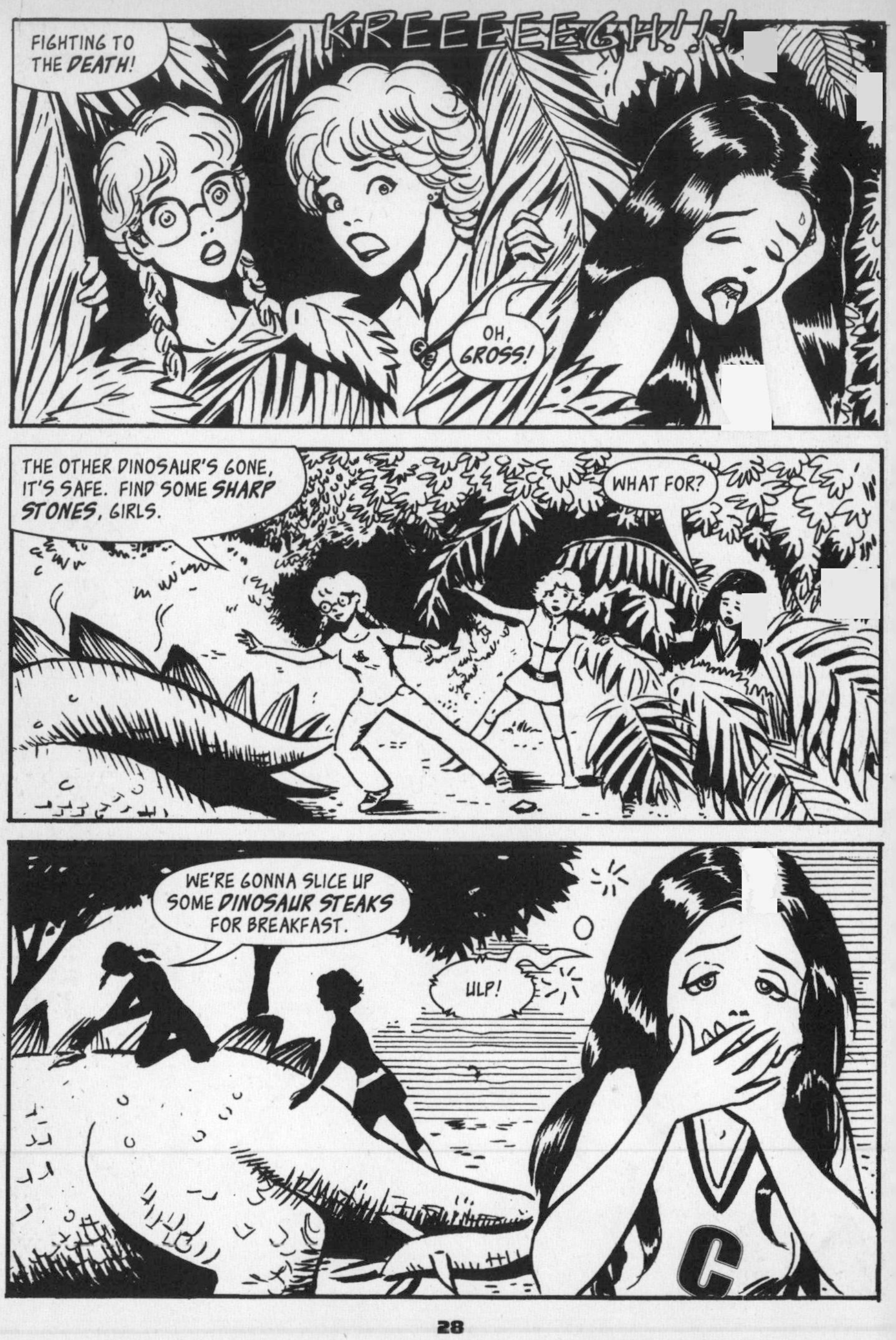
KREEEEEEGH!!!
FIGHTING TO THE DEATH!
OH, GROSS!
THE OTHER DINOSAUR'S GONE, IT'S SAFE. FIND SOME SHARP STONES, GIRLS.
WHAT FOR?
WE'RE GONNA SLICE UP SOME DINOSAUR STEAKS FOR BREAKFAST.
ULP!

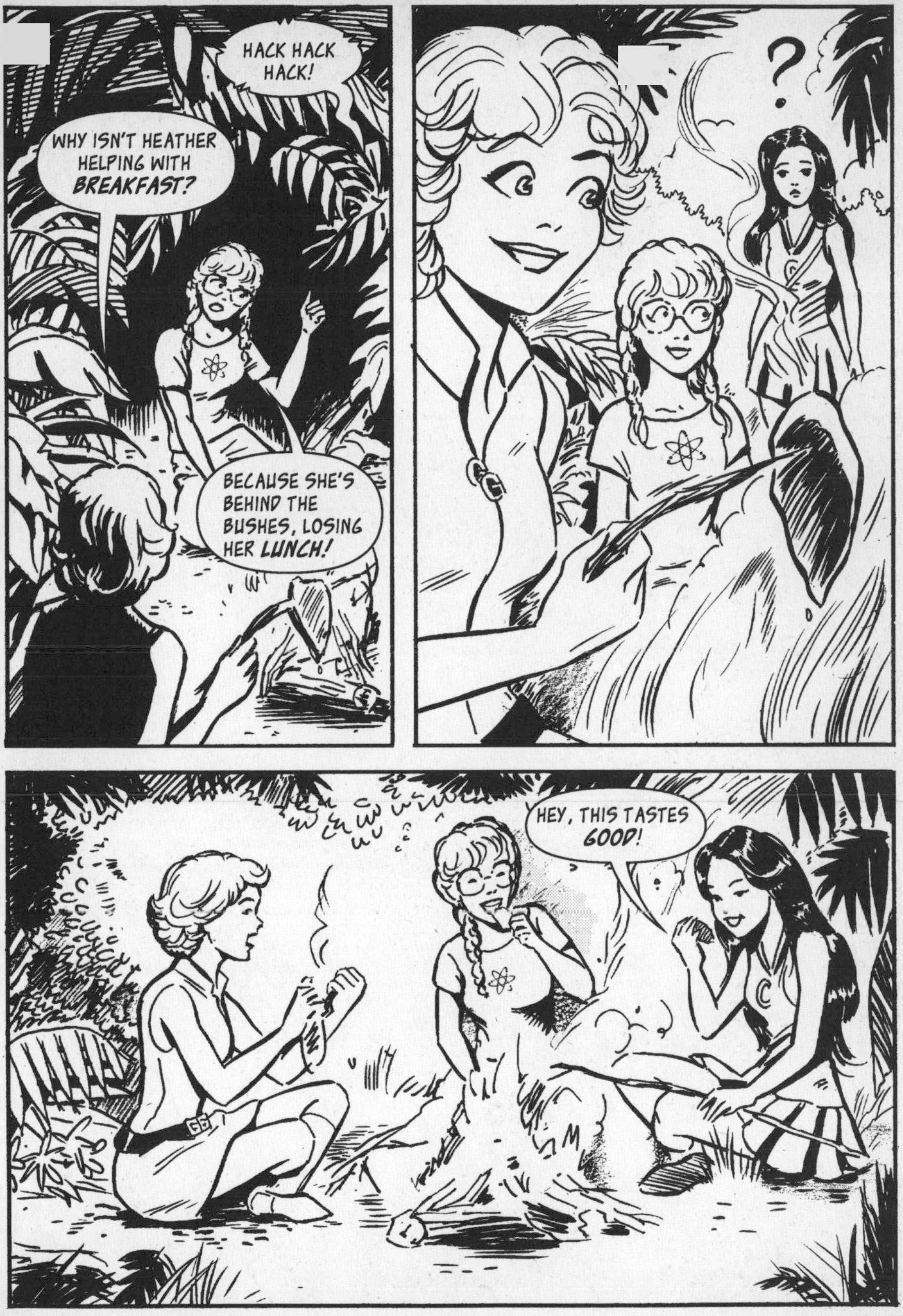
HACK HACK HACK!
WHY ISN'T HEATHER HELPING WITH *BREAKFAST?*
BECAUSE SHE'S BEHIND THE BUSHES, LOSING HER *LUNCH!*
?
HEY, THIS TASTES *GOOD!*

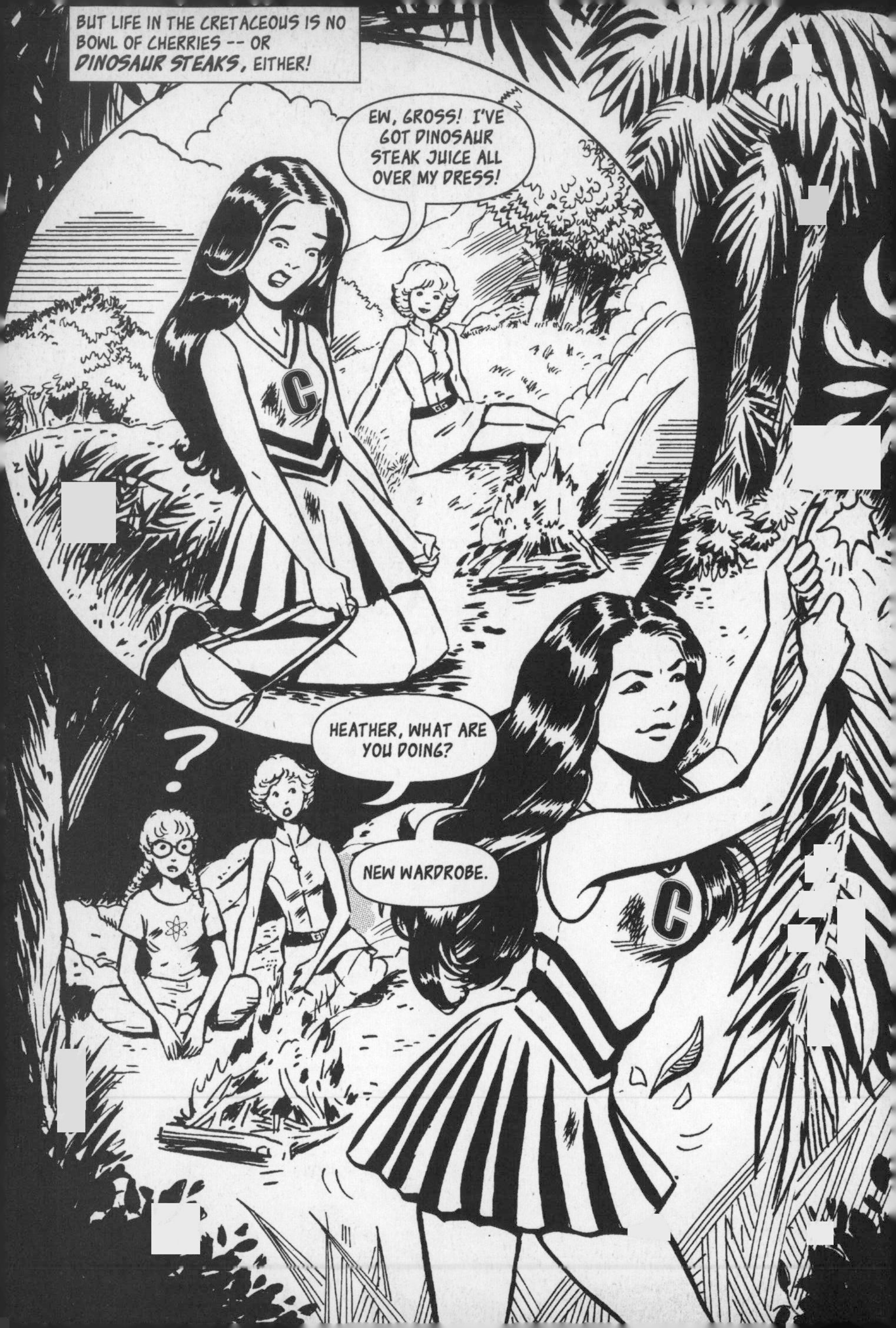
BUT LIFE IN THE CRETACEOUS IS NO BOWL OF CHERRIES -- OR DINOSAUR STEAKS, EITHER!
EW, GROSS! I'VE GOT DINOSAUR STEAK JUICE ALL OVER MY DRESS!
?
HEATHER, WHAT ARE YOU DOING?
NEW WARDROBE.

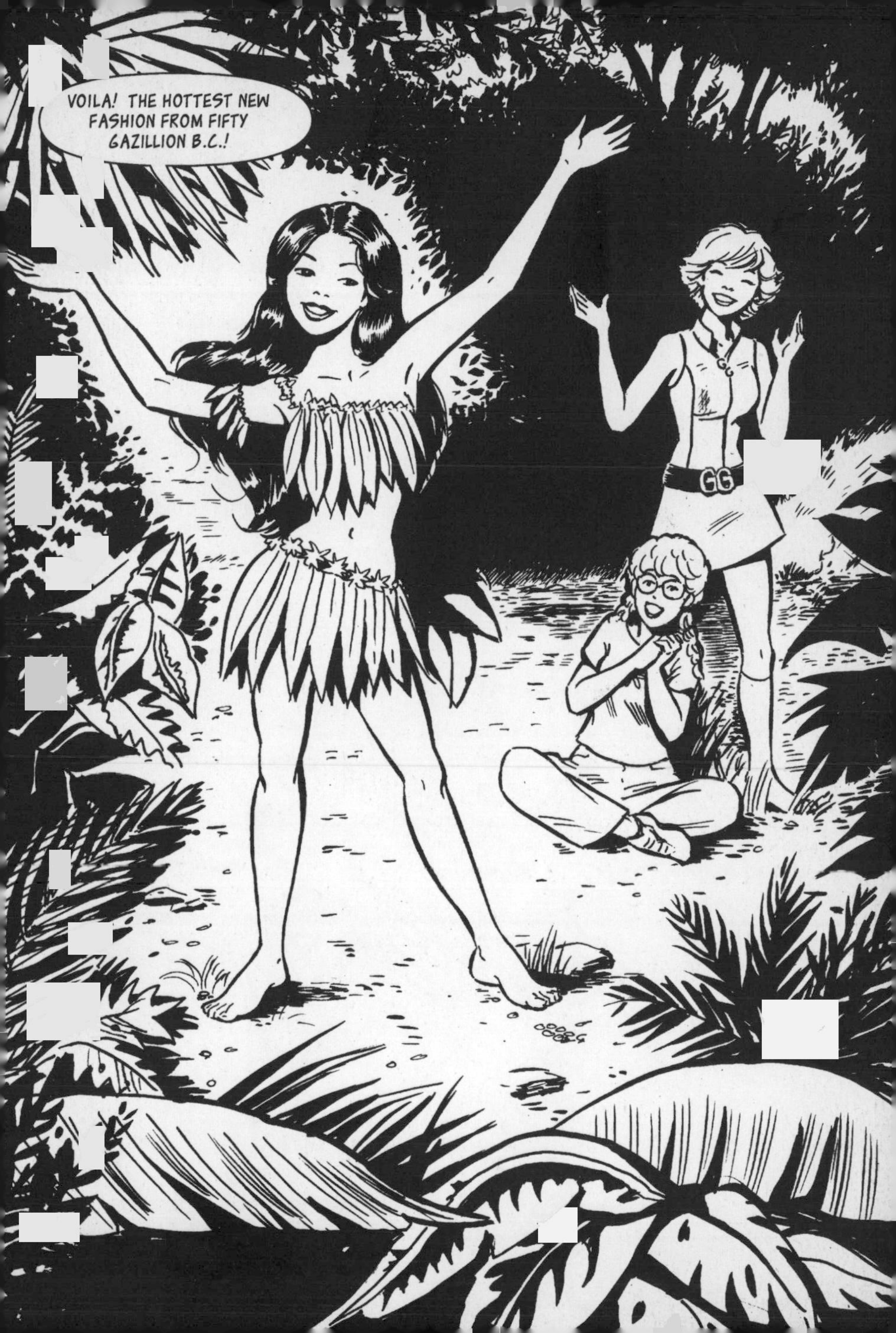
VOILA! THE HOTTEST NEW FASHION FROM FIFTY GAZILLION B.C.!

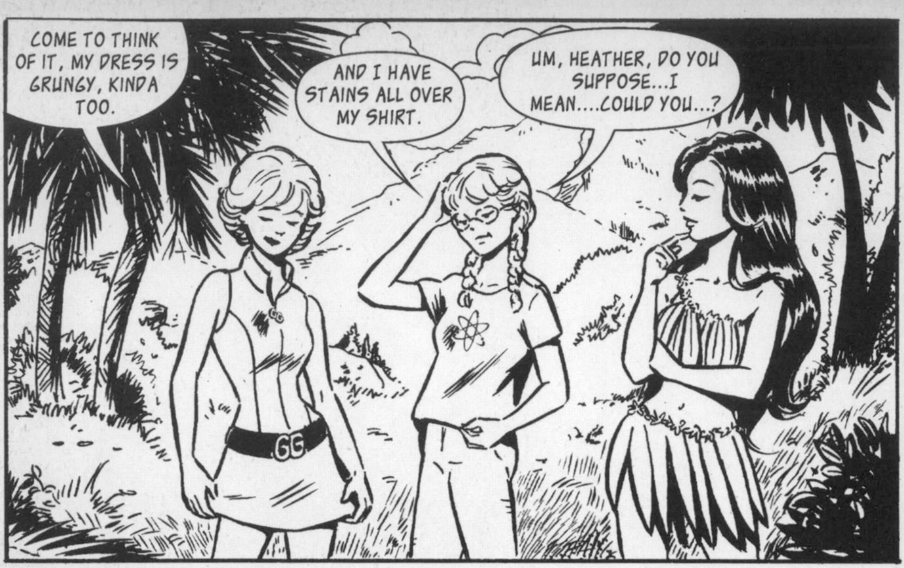

COME TO THINK OF IT, MY DRESS IS GRUNGY, KINDA TOO.
AND I HAVE STAINS ALL OVER MY SHIRT.
UM, HEATHER, DO YOU SUPPOSE...I MEAN....COULD YOU...?

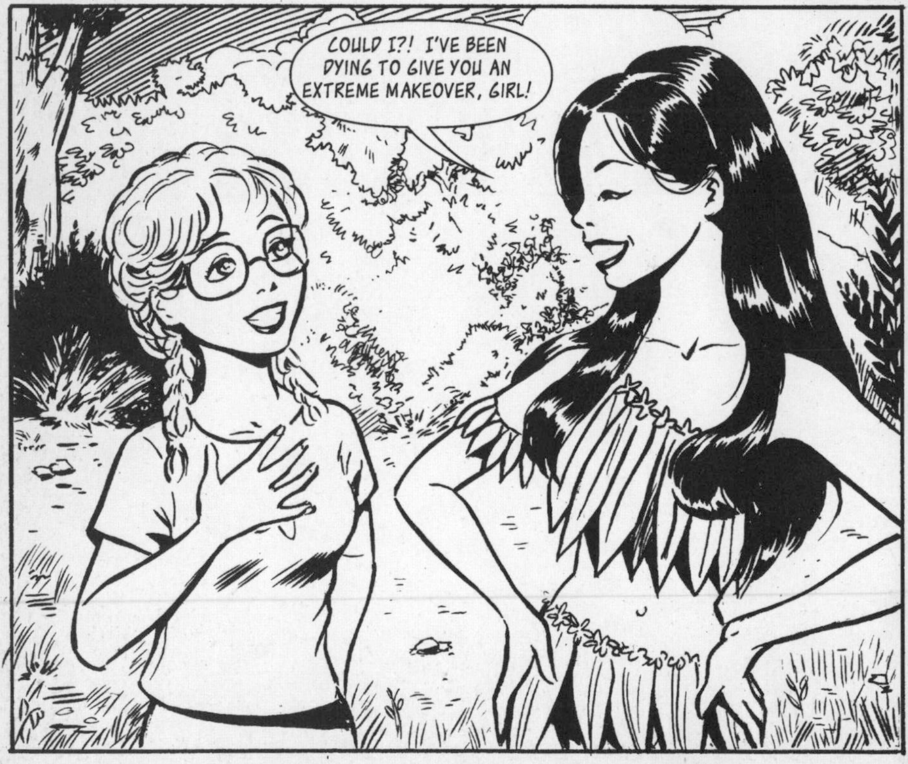

COULD I?! I'VE BEEN DYING TO GIVE YOU AN EXTREME MAKEOVER, GIRL!

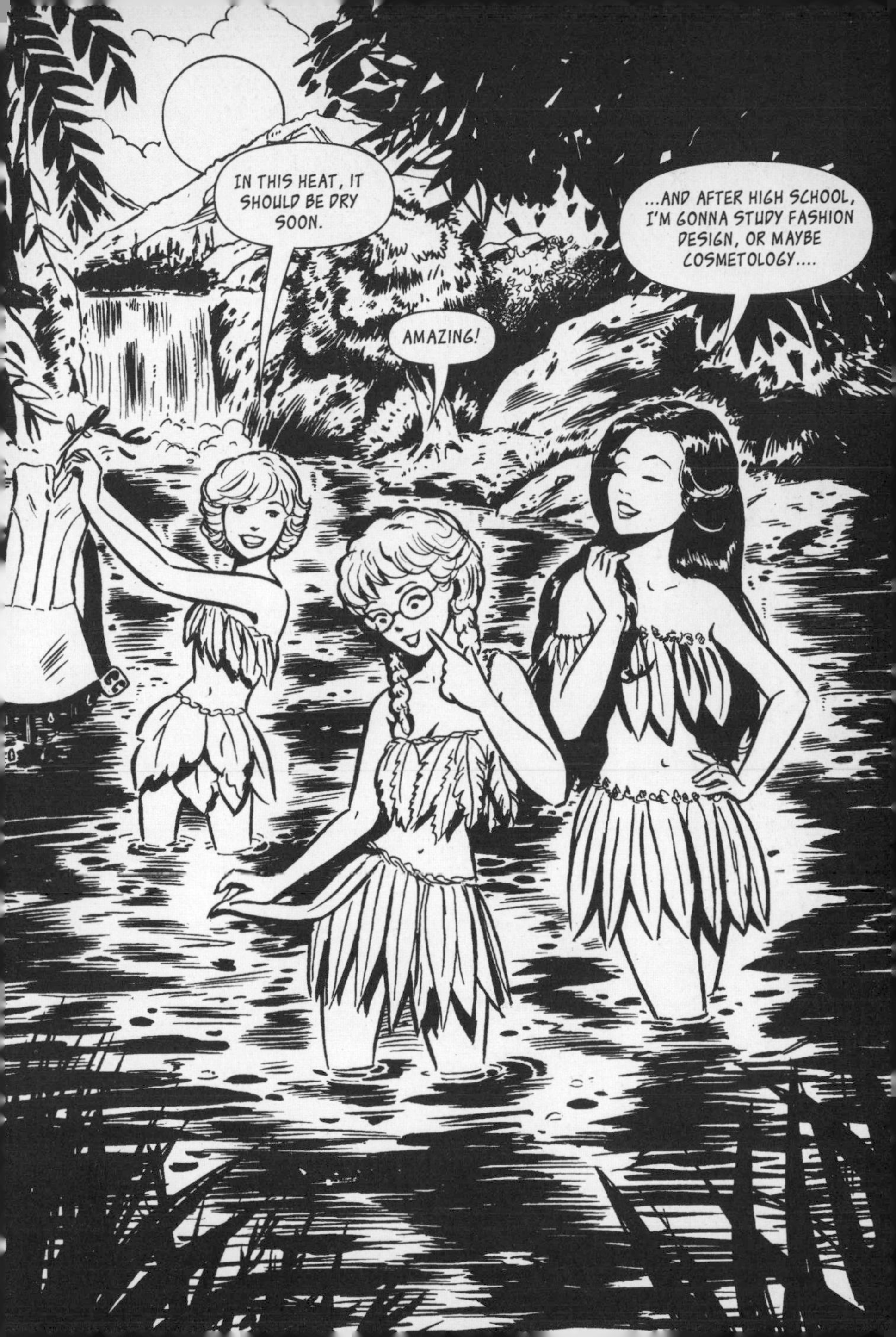
IN THIS HEAT, IT SHOULD BE DRY SOON.
AMAZING!
...AND AFTER HIGH SCHOOL, I'M GONNA STUDY FASHION DESIGN, OR MAYBE COSMETOLOGY....

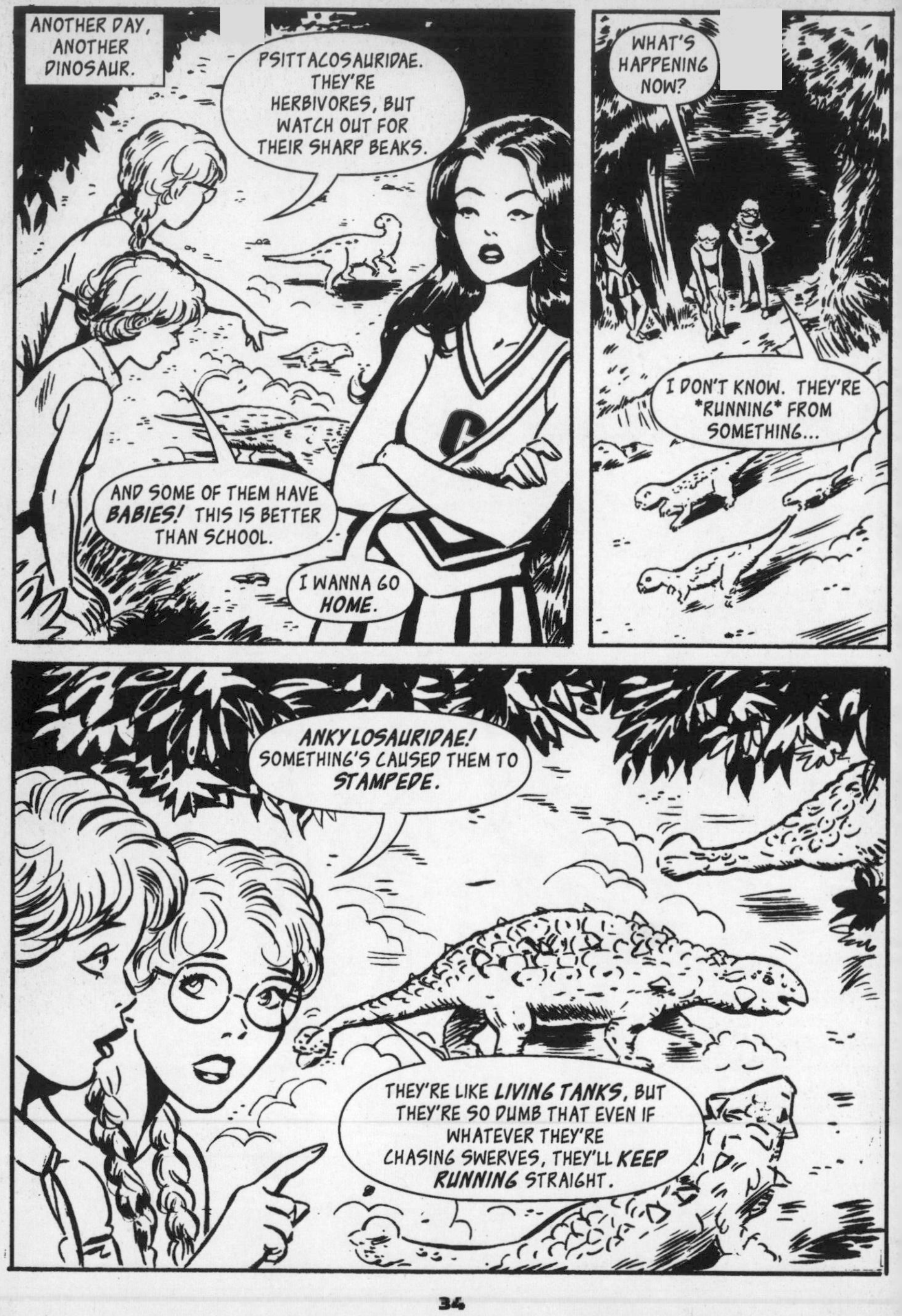
ANOTHER DAY, ANOTHER DINOSAUR.
PSITTACOSAURIDAE. THEY'RE HERBIVORES, BUT WATCH OUT FOR THEIR SHARP BEAKS.
AND SOME OF THEM HAVE BABIES! THIS IS BETTER THAN SCHOOL.
I WANNA GO HOME.
WHAT'S HAPPENING NOW?
I DON'T KNOW. THEY'RE *RUNNING* FROM SOMETHING...
ANKYLOSAURIDAE! SOMETHING'S CAUSED THEM TO STAMPEDE.
THEY'RE LIKE LIVING TANKS, BUT THEY'RE SO DUMB THAT EVEN IF WHATEVER THEY'RE CHASING SWERVES, THEY'LL KEEP RUNNING STRAIGHT.

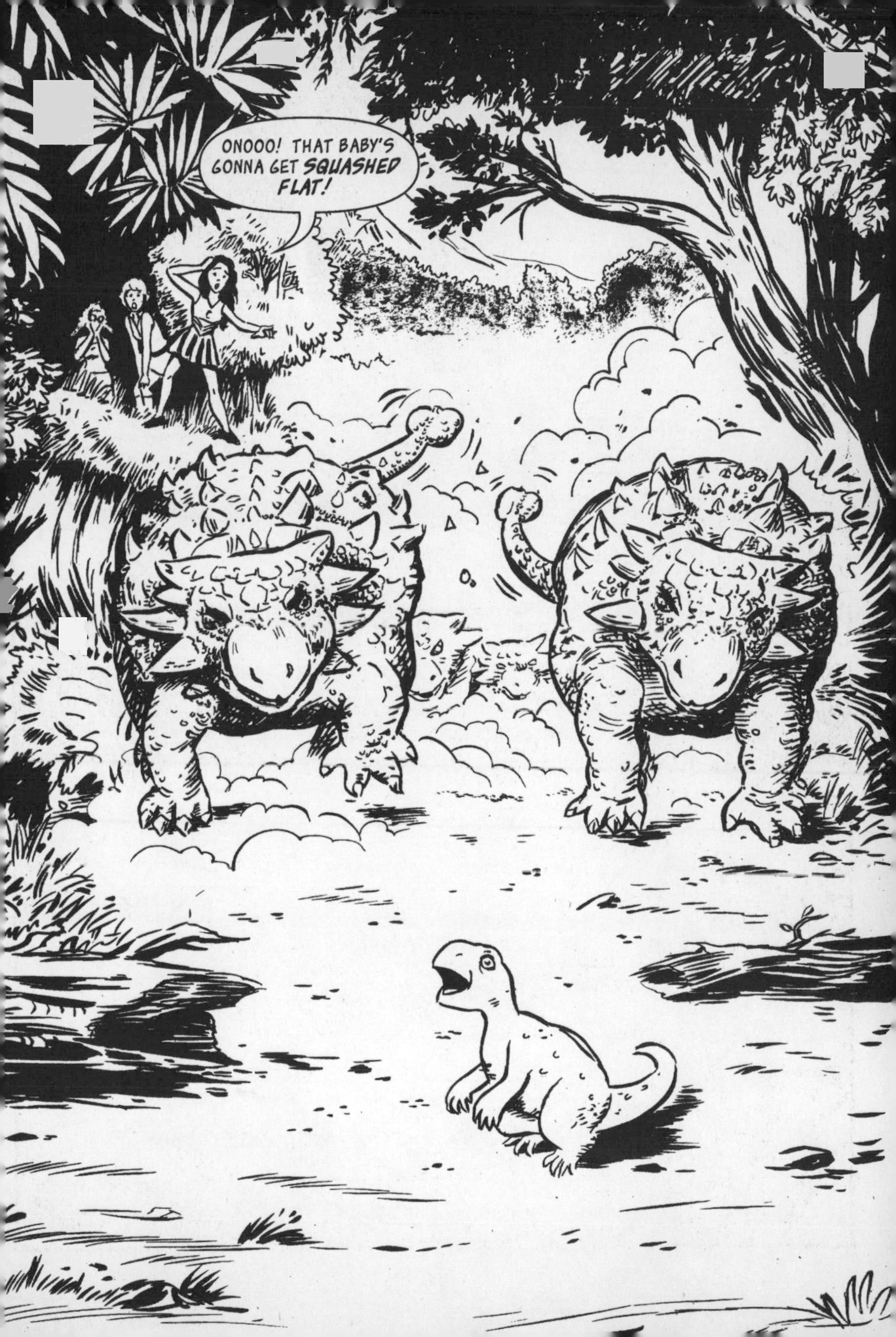
ONOOO! THAT BABY'S GONNA GET SQUASHED FLAT!

YAY, LINDSAY!
YOU GO, GIRL!
GOTCHA, LITTLE GUY!
OOH, HE'S SO CUTE!
I THINK HE LIKES ME.

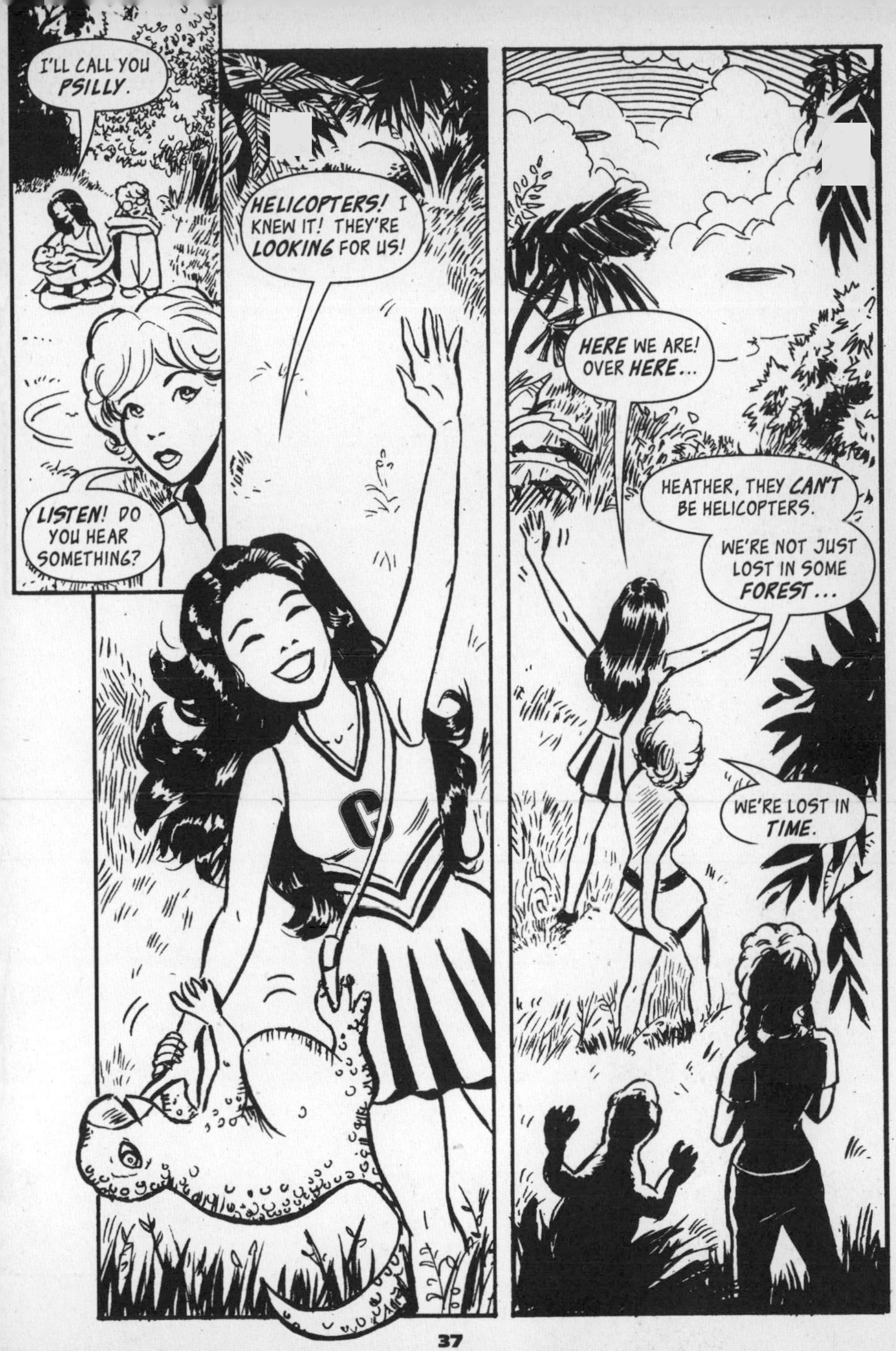
I'LL CALL YOU PSILLY.
LISTEN! DO YOU HEAR SOMETHING?
HELICOPTERS! I KNEW IT! THEY'RE LOOKING FOR US!
HERE WE ARE! OVER HERE...
HEATHER, THEY CAN'T BE HELICOPTERS.
WE'RE NOT JUST LOST IN SOME FOREST...
WE'RE LOST IN TIME.

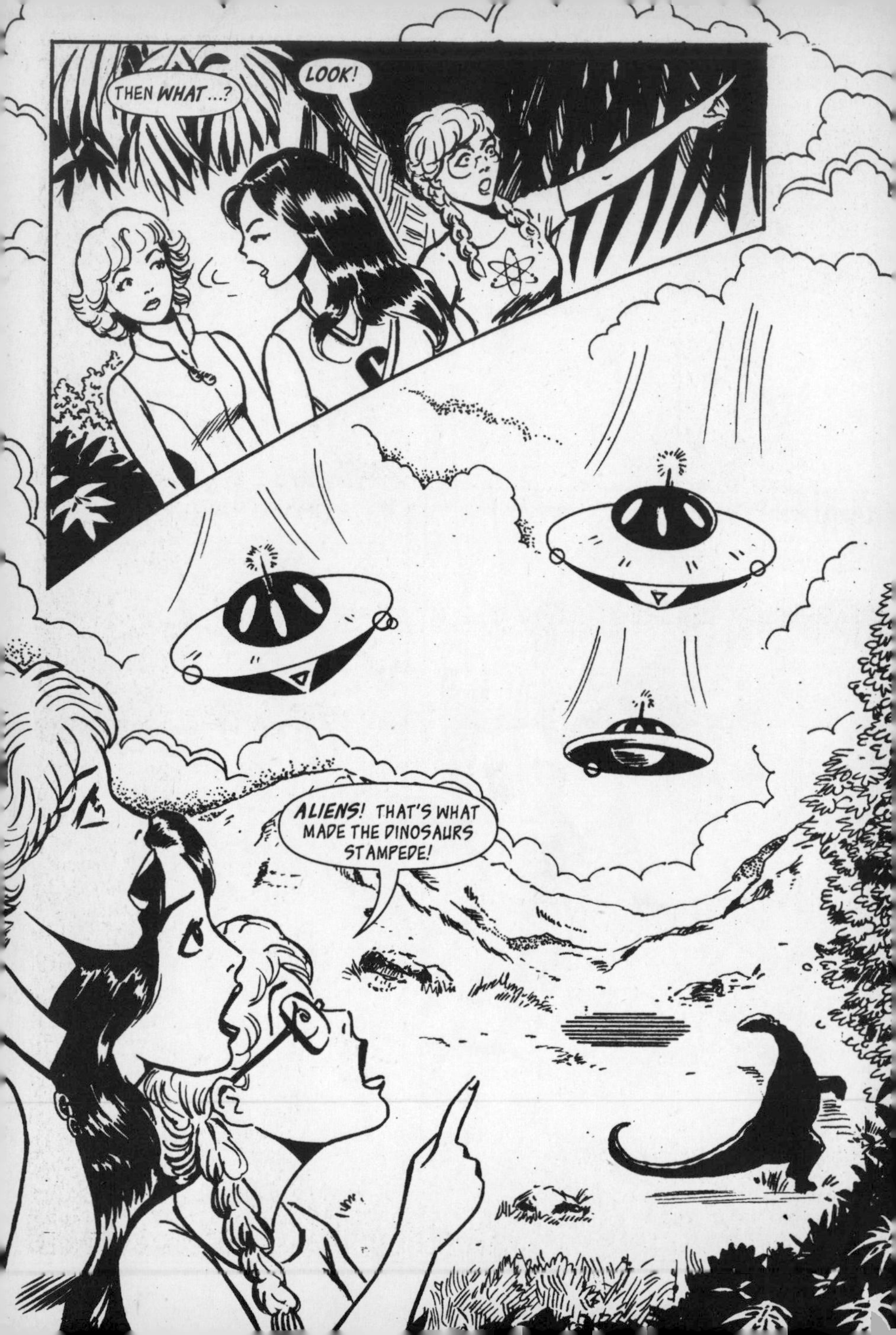
THEN WHAT...?
LOOK!
ALIENS! THAT'S WHAT MADE THE DINOSAURS STAMPEDE!

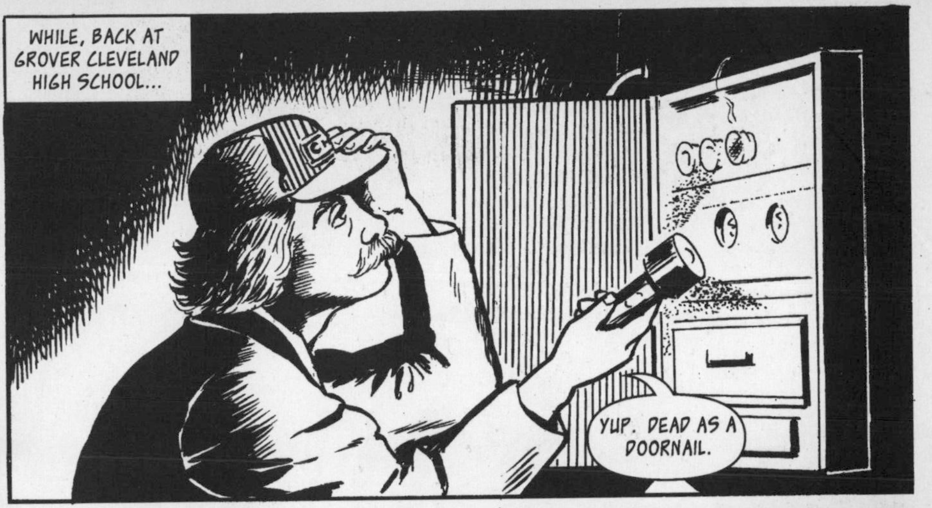
WHILE, BACK AT GROVER CLEVELAND HIGH SCHOOL...
YUP. DEAD AS A DOORNAIL.

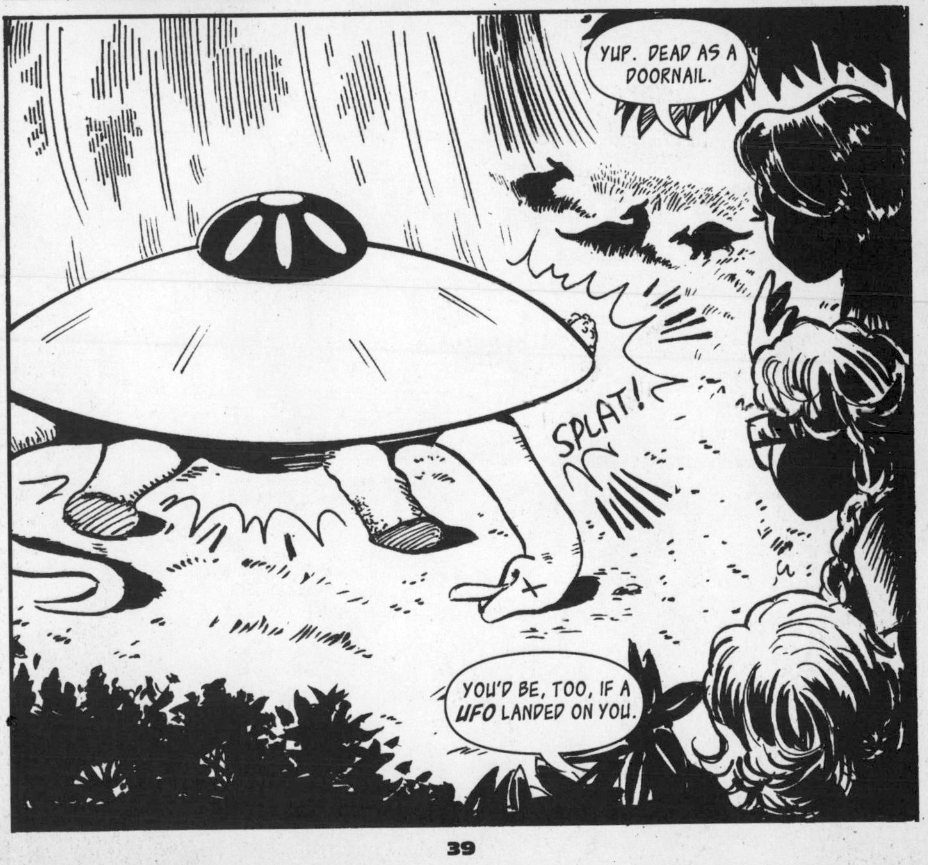
YUP. DEAD AS A DOORNAIL.
SPLAT!
YOU'D BE, TOO, IF A UFO LANDED ON YOU.

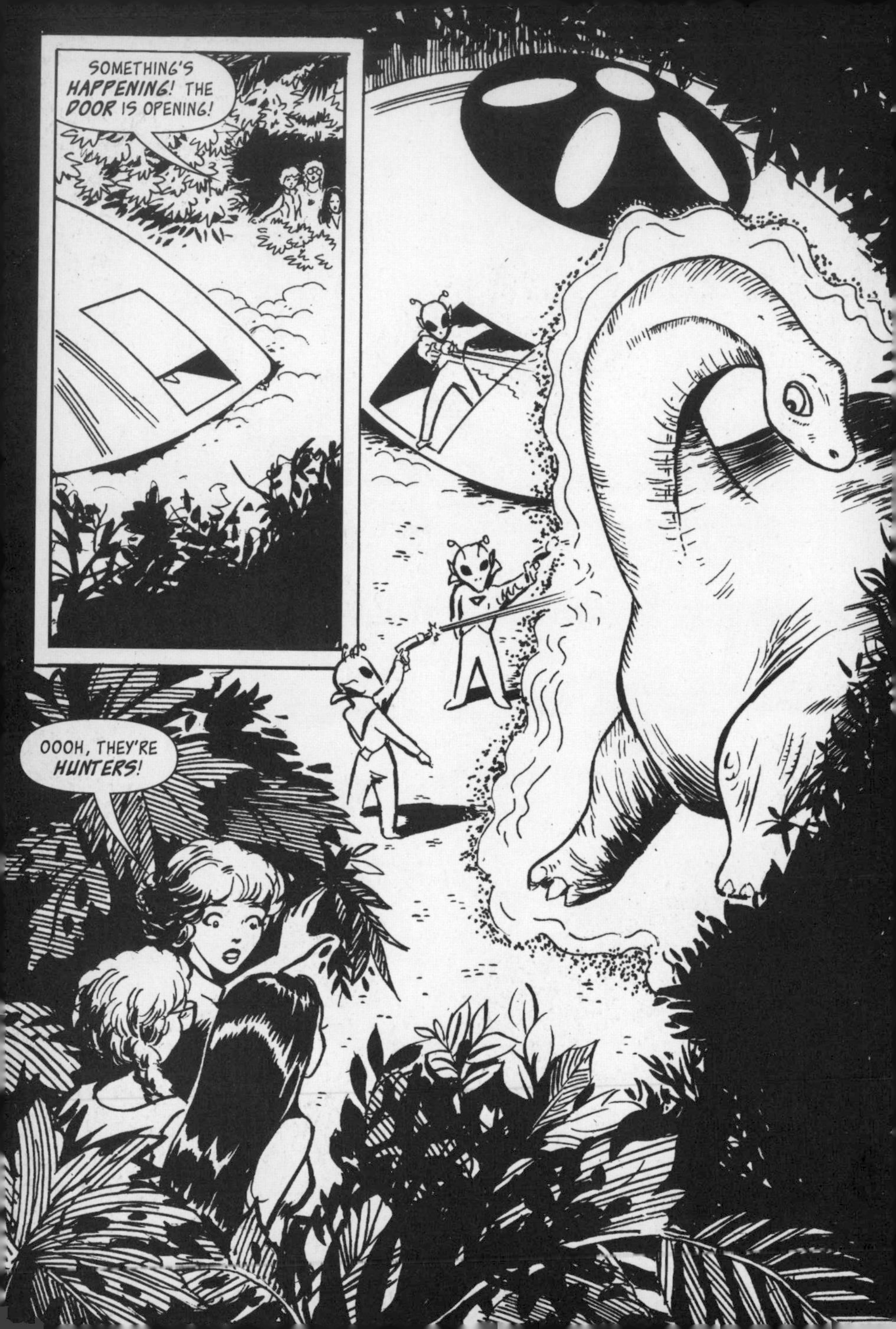
SOMETHING'S HAPPENING! THE DOOR IS OPENING!
OOOH, THEY'RE HUNTERS!

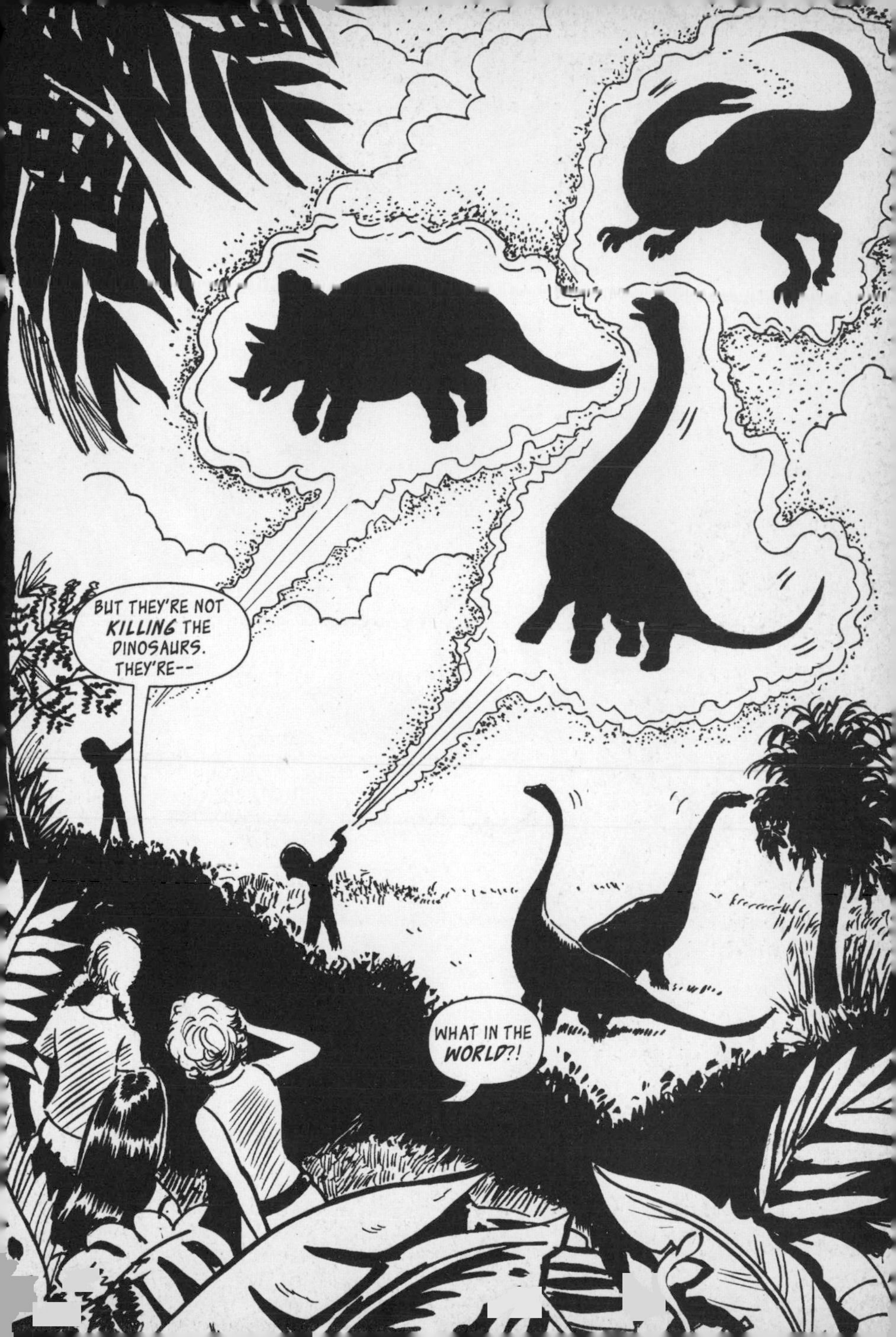
BUT THEY'RE NOT *KILLING* THE DINOSAURS. THEY'RE--
WHAT IN THE *WORLD*?!

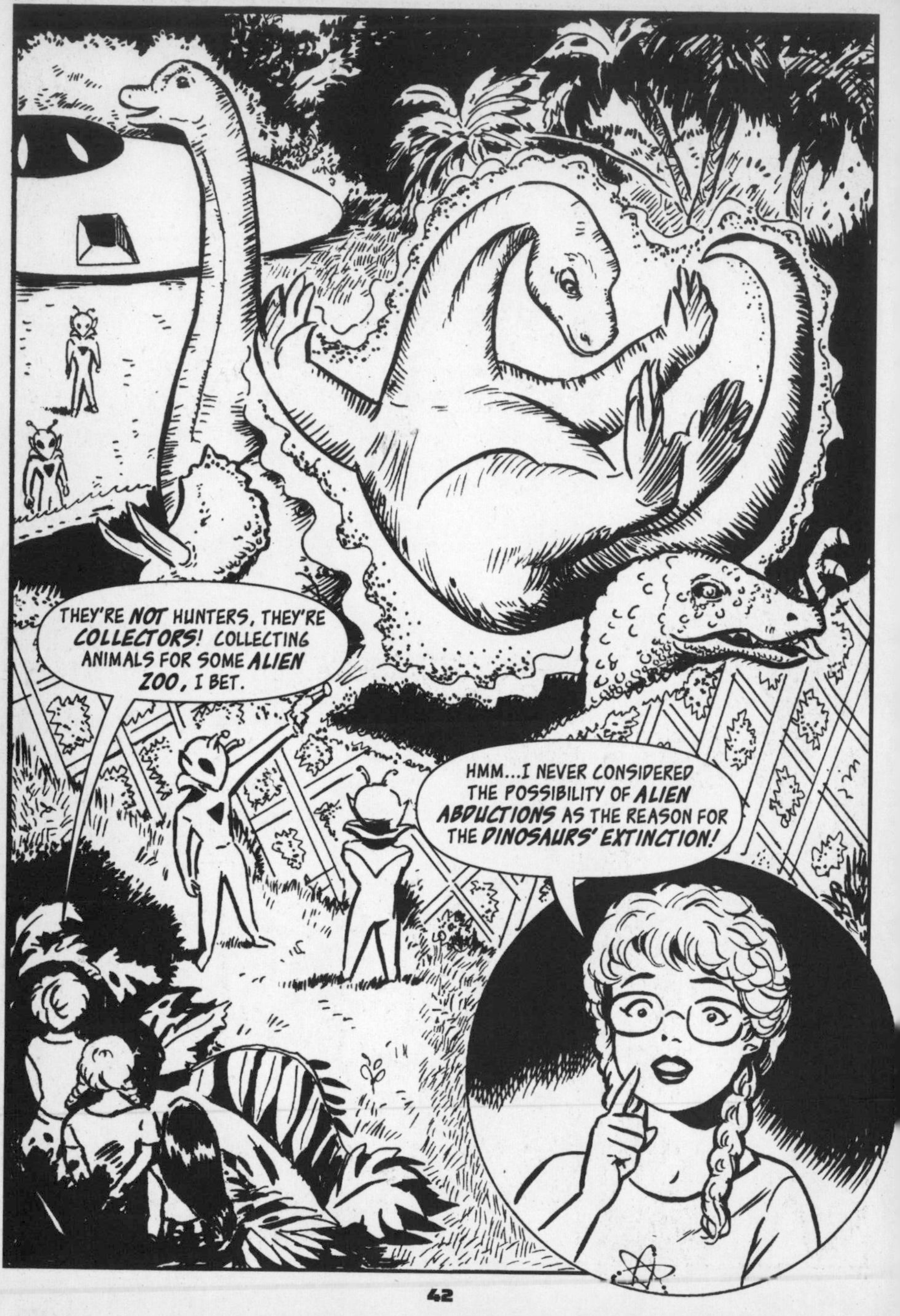
THEY'RE NOT HUNTERS, THEY'RE COLLECTORS! COLLECTING ANIMALS FOR SOME ALIEN ZOO, I BET.
HMM...I NEVER CONSIDERED THE POSSIBILITY OF ALIEN ABDUCTIONS AS THE REASON FOR THE DINOSAURS' EXTINCTION!

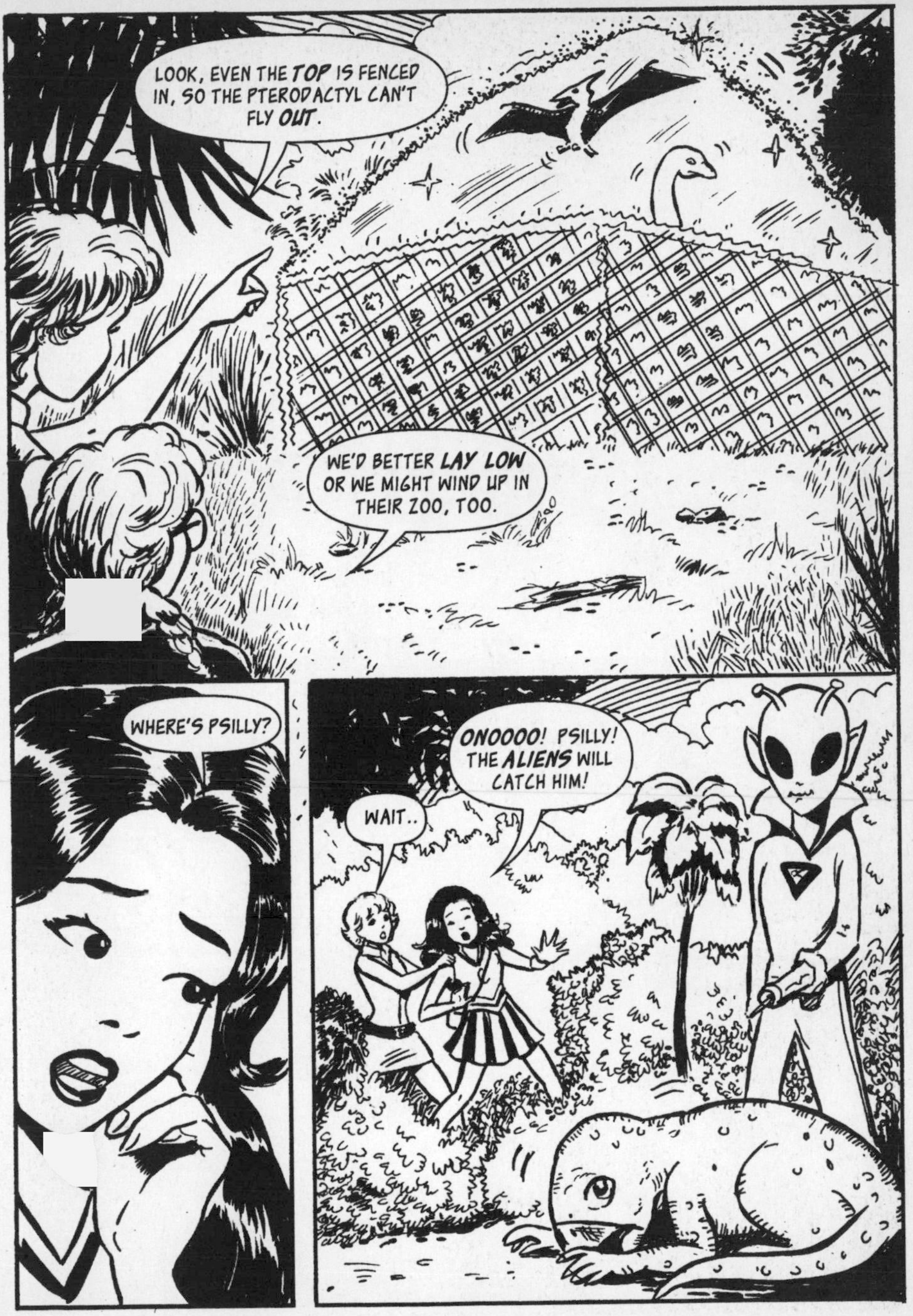
LOOK, EVEN THE TOP IS FENCED IN, SO THE PTERODACTYL CAN'T FLY OUT.
WE'D BETTER LAY LOW OR WE MIGHT WIND UP IN THEIR ZOO, TOO.
WHERE'S PSILLY?
WAIT..
ONOOOO! PSILLY! THE ALIENS WILL CATCH HIM!

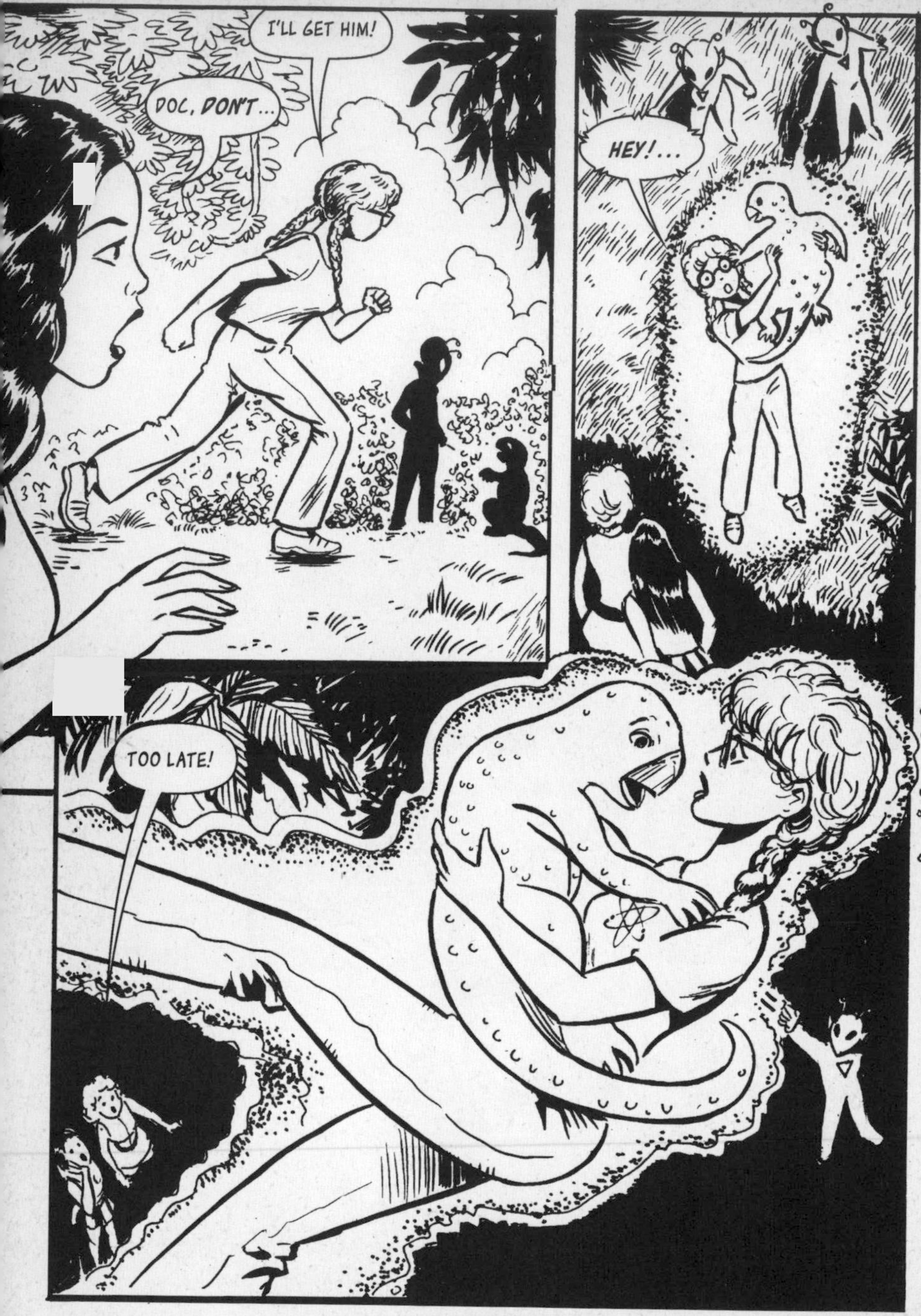
I'LL GET HIM!
DOC, DON'T...
HEY!...
TOO LATE!

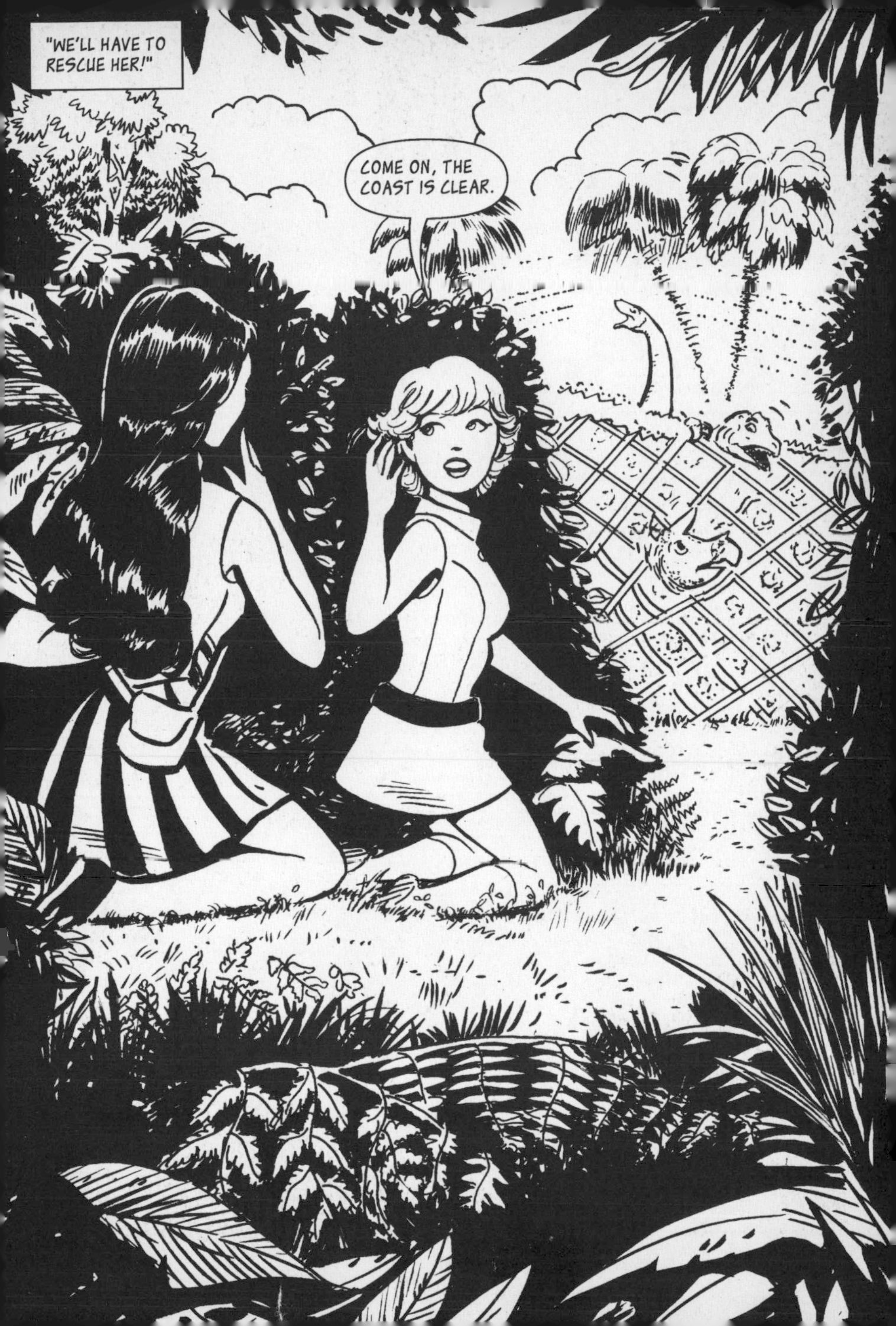
"WE'LL HAVE TO RESCUE HER!"
COME ON, THE COAST IS CLEAR.

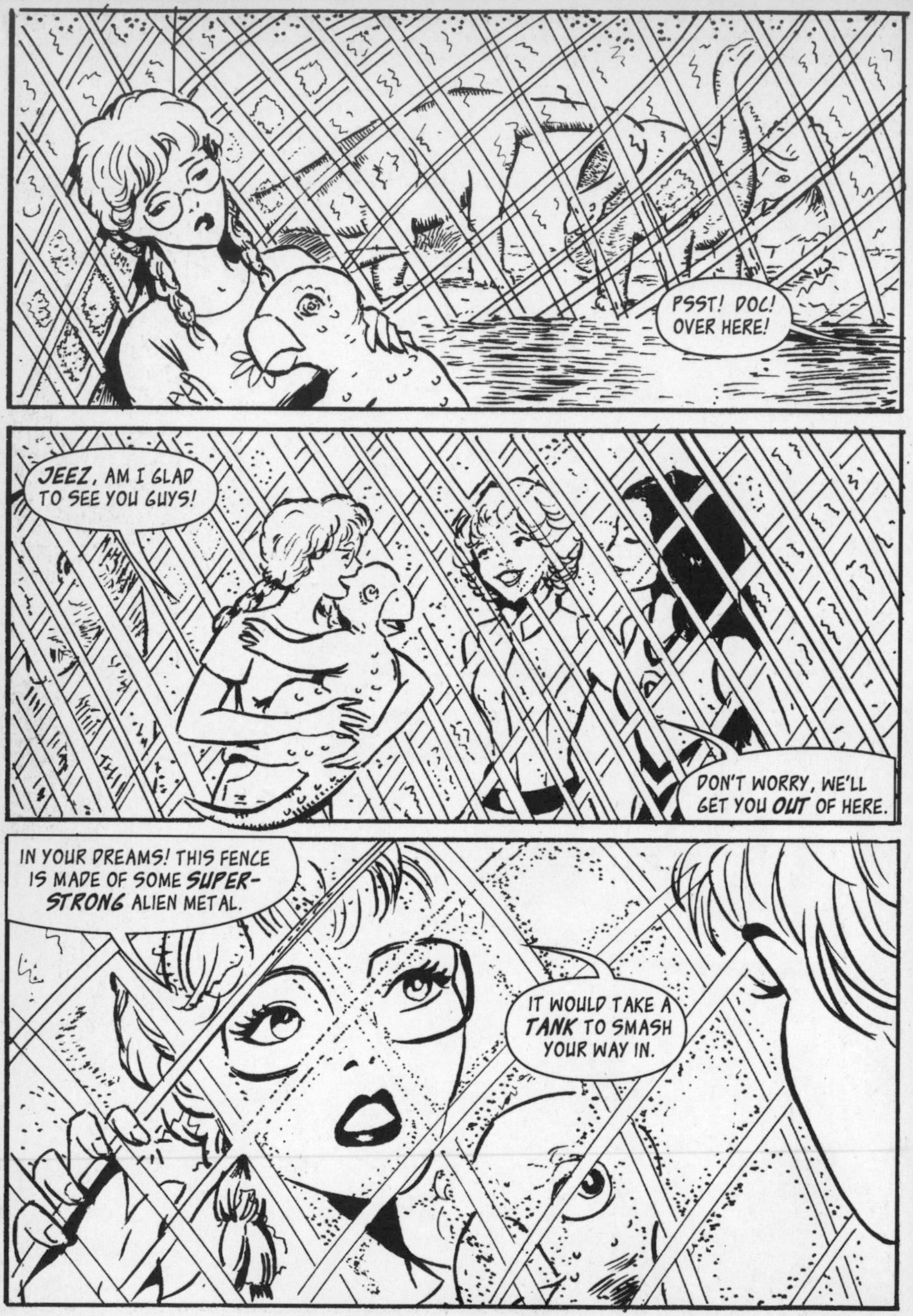
PSST! DOC! OVER HERE!
JEEZ, AM I GLAD TO SEE YOU GUYS!
DON'T WORRY, WE'LL GET YOU OUT OF HERE.
IN YOUR DREAMS! THIS FENCE IS MADE OF SOME SUPER-STRONG ALIEN METAL.
IT WOULD TAKE A TANK TO SMASH YOUR WAY IN.

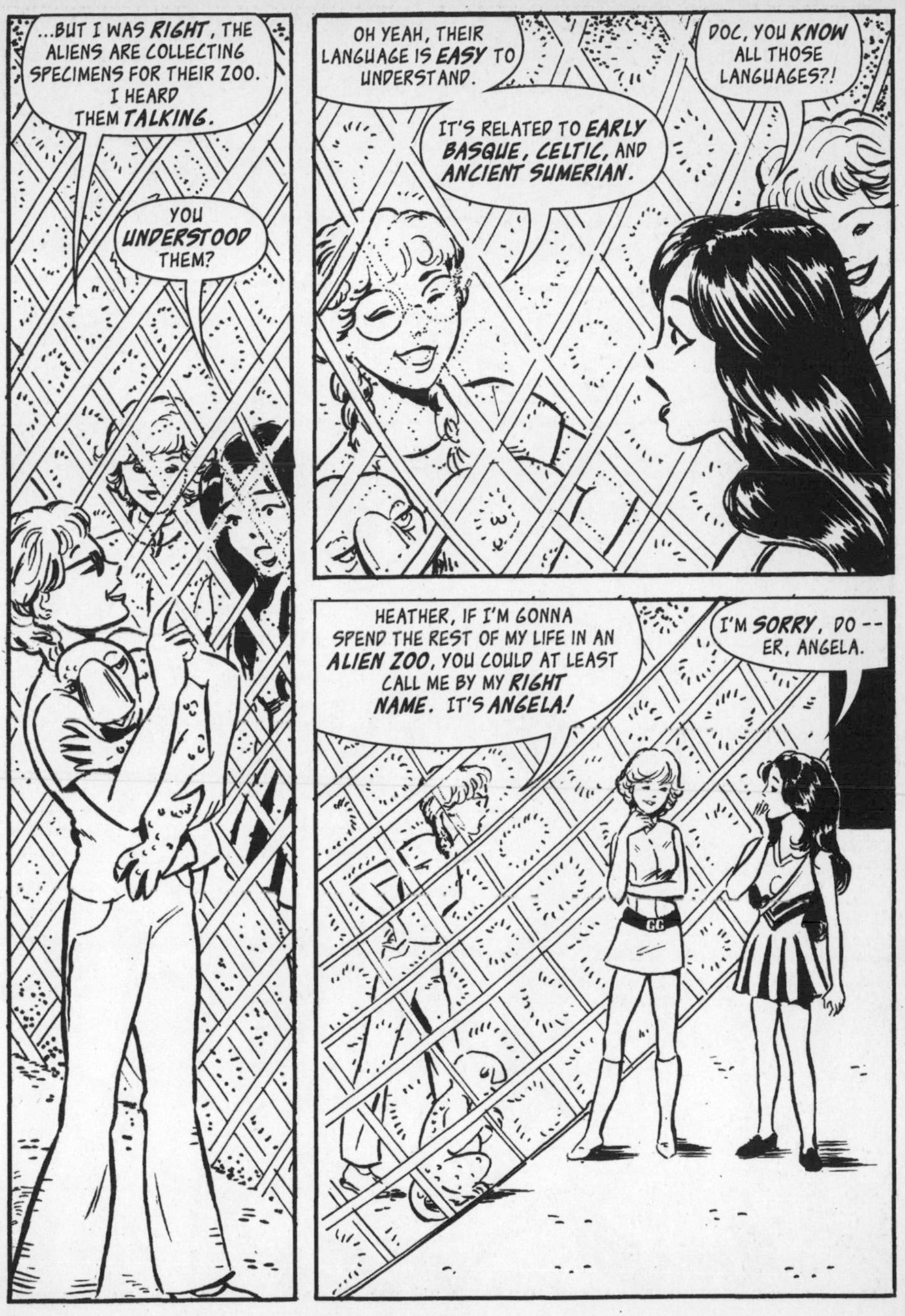
...BUT I WAS RIGHT, THE ALIENS ARE COLLECTING SPECIMENS FOR THEIR ZOO. I HEARD THEM TALKING.
YOU UNDERSTOOD THEM?
OH YEAH, THEIR LANGUAGE IS EASY TO UNDERSTAND.
IT'S RELATED TO EARLY BASQUE, CELTIC, AND ANCIENT SUMERIAN.
DOC, YOU KNOW ALL THOSE LANGUAGES?!
HEATHER, IF I'M GONNA SPEND THE REST OF MY LIFE IN AN ALIEN ZOO, YOU COULD AT LEAST CALL ME BY MY RIGHT NAME. IT'S ANGELA!
I'M SORRY, DO -- ER, ANGELA.

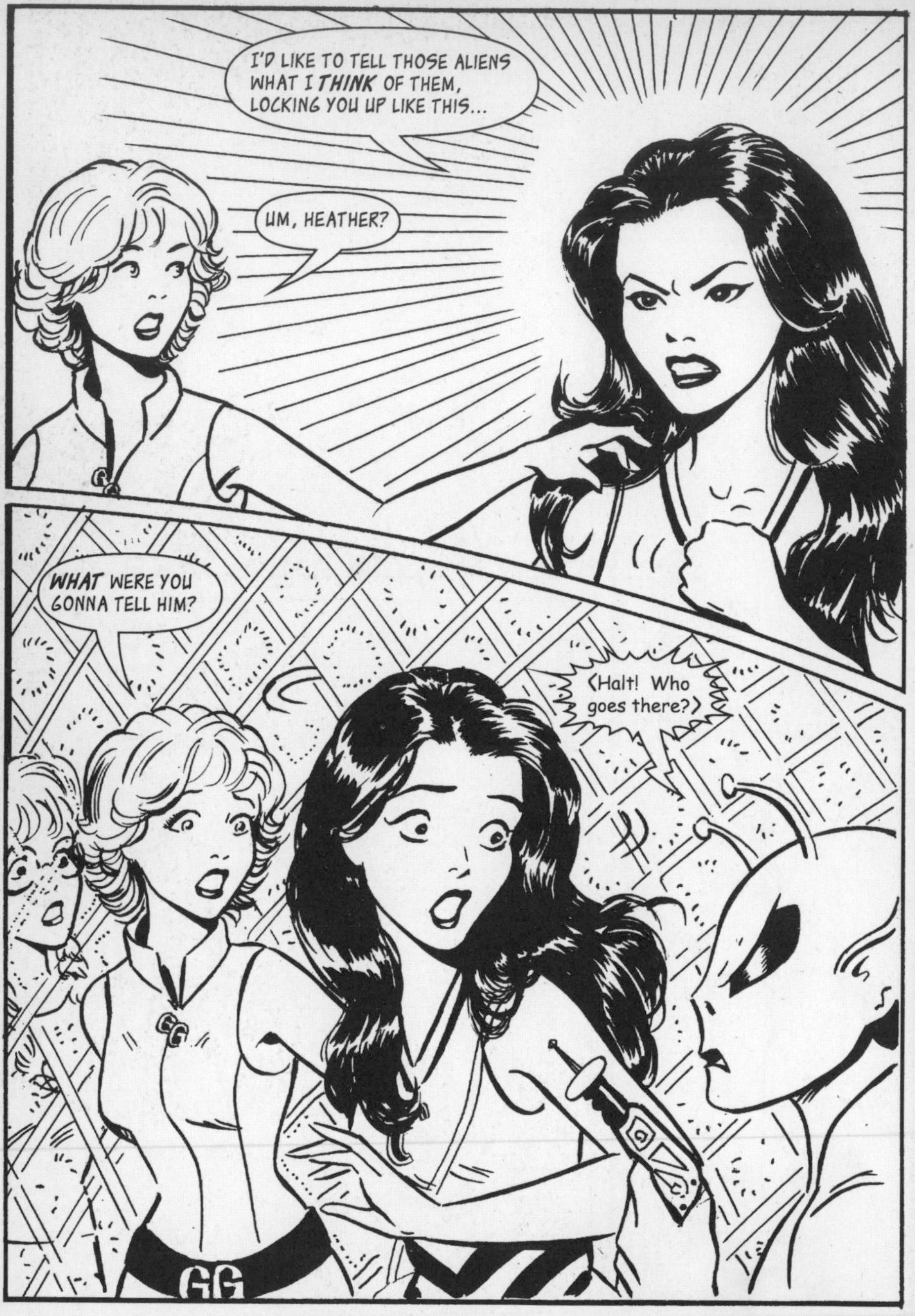
I'D LIKE TO TELL THOSE ALIENS WHAT I *THINK* OF THEM, LOCKING YOU UP LIKE THIS...
UM, HEATHER?
WHAT WERE YOU GONNA TELL HIM?
‹Halt! Who goes there?›

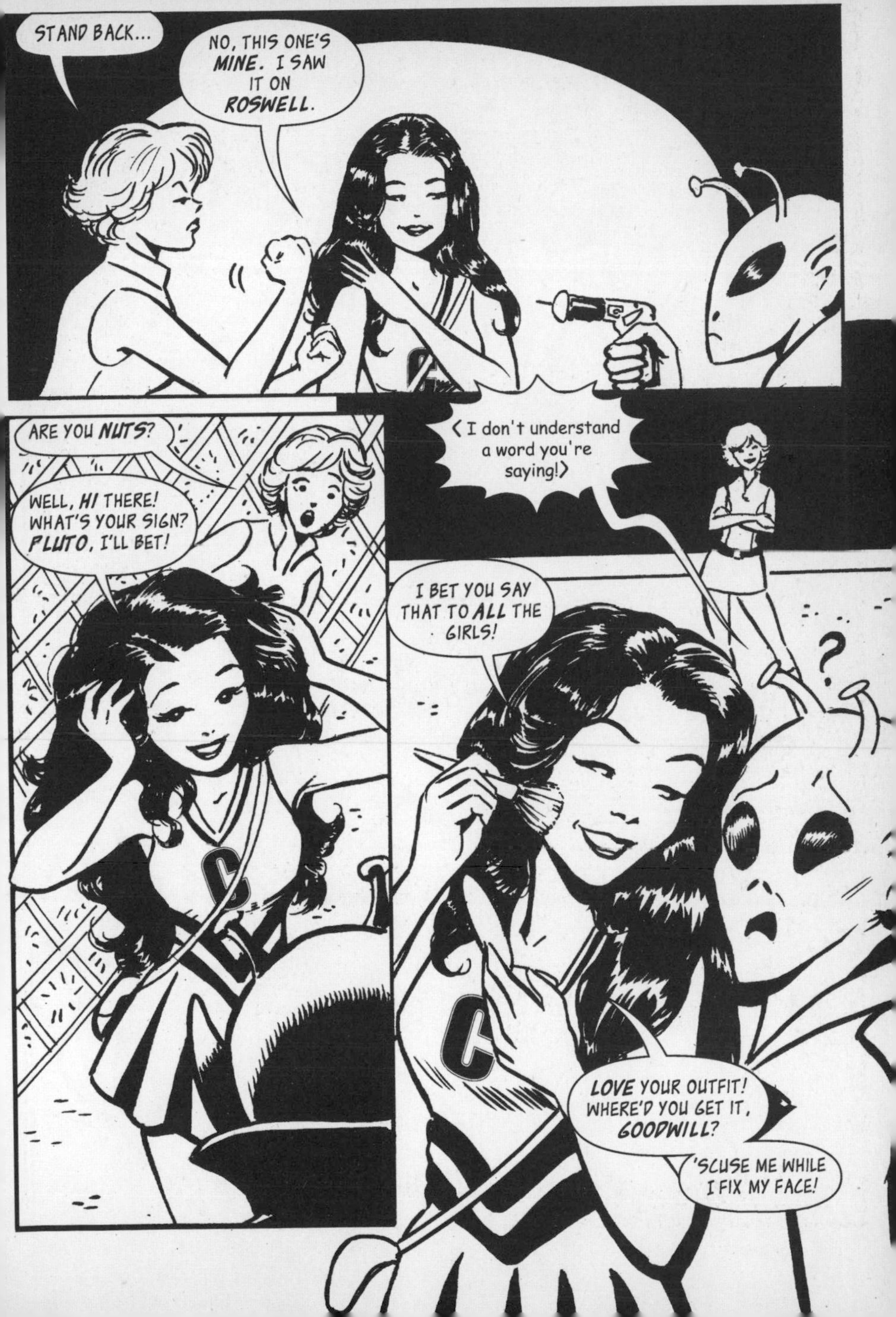
STAND BACK...
NO, THIS ONE'S MINE. I SAW IT ON ROSWELL.
ARE YOU NUTS?
WELL, HI THERE! WHAT'S YOUR SIGN? PLUTO, I'LL BET!
‹I don't understand a word you're saying!›
I BET YOU SAY THAT TO ALL THE GIRLS!
?
LOVE YOUR OUTFIT! WHERE'D YOU GET IT, GOODWILL?
'SCUSE ME WHILE I FIX MY FACE!

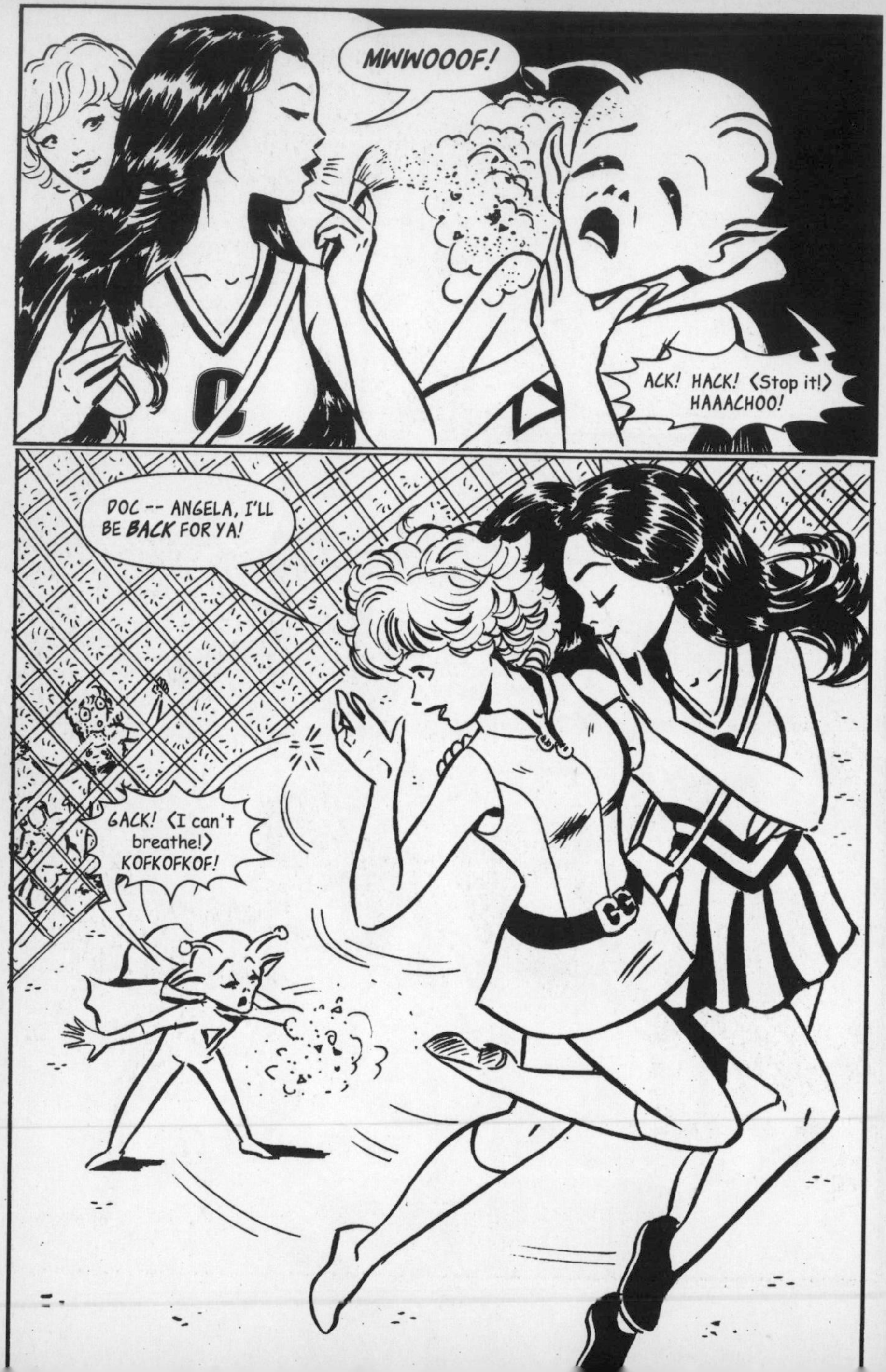
MWWOOOF!
ACK! HACK! <Stop it!> HAAACHOO!
DOC -- ANGELA, I'LL BE BACK FOR YA!
GACK! <I can't breathe!> KOFKOFKOF!

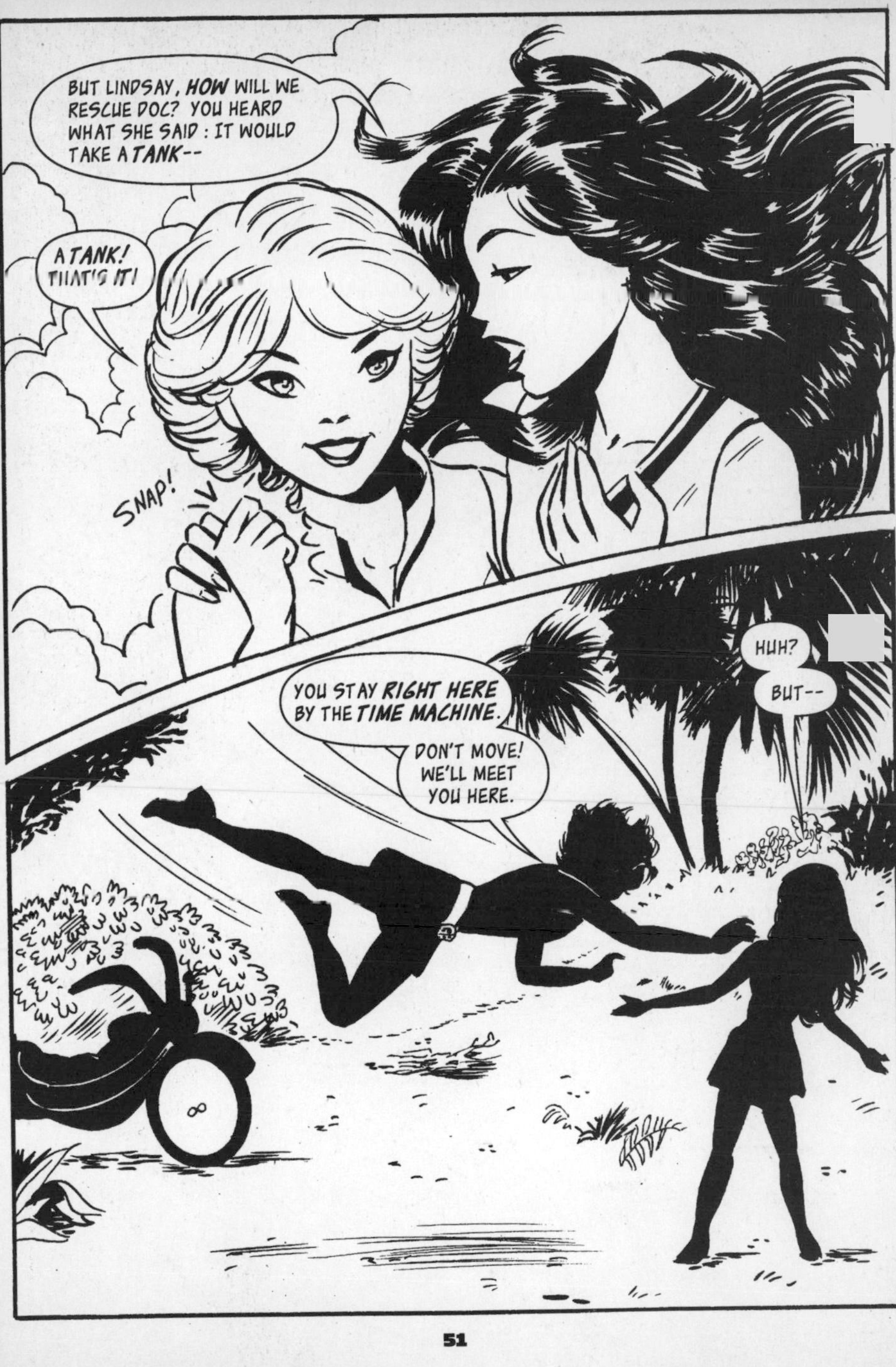
BUT LINDSAY, HOW WILL WE RESCUE DOC? YOU HEARD WHAT SHE SAID : IT WOULD TAKE A TANK--
A TANK! THAT'S IT!
SNAP!
YOU STAY RIGHT HERE BY THE TIME MACHINE.
DON'T MOVE! WE'LL MEET YOU HERE.
HUH?
BUT--

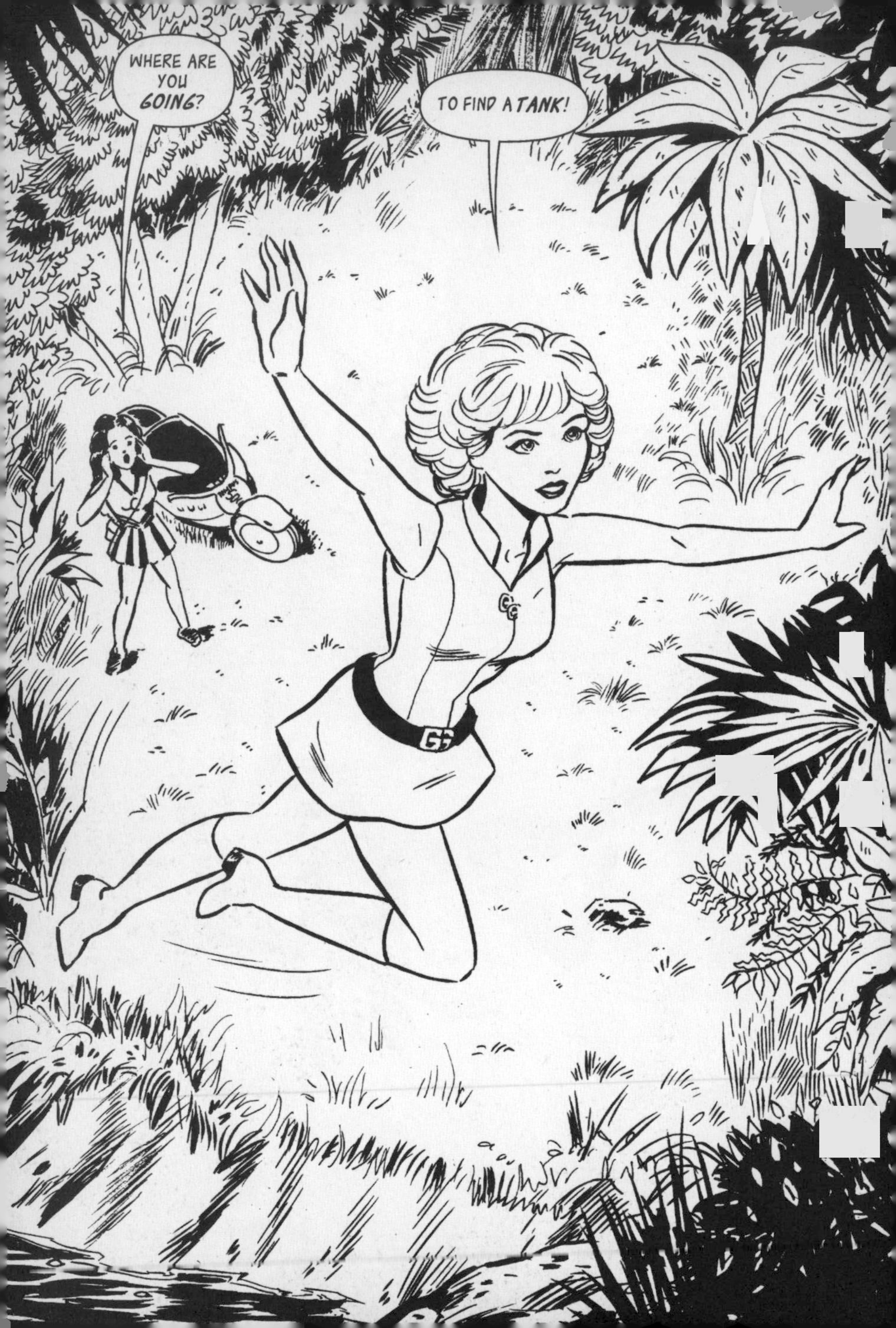
WHERE ARE YOU GOING?
TO FIND A TANK!

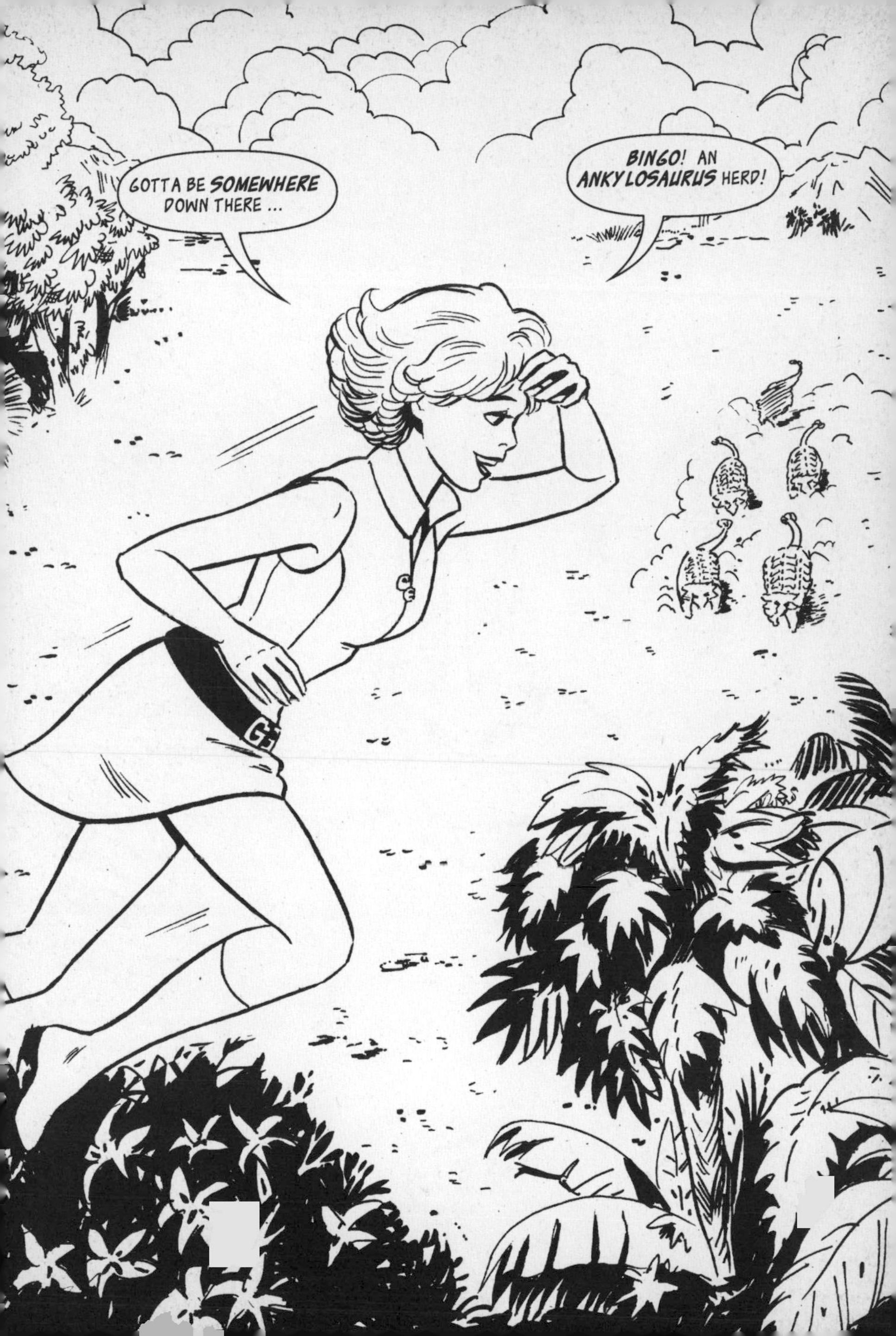
GOTTA BE SOMEWHERE DOWN THERE ...
BINGO! AN ANKYLOSAURUS HERD!

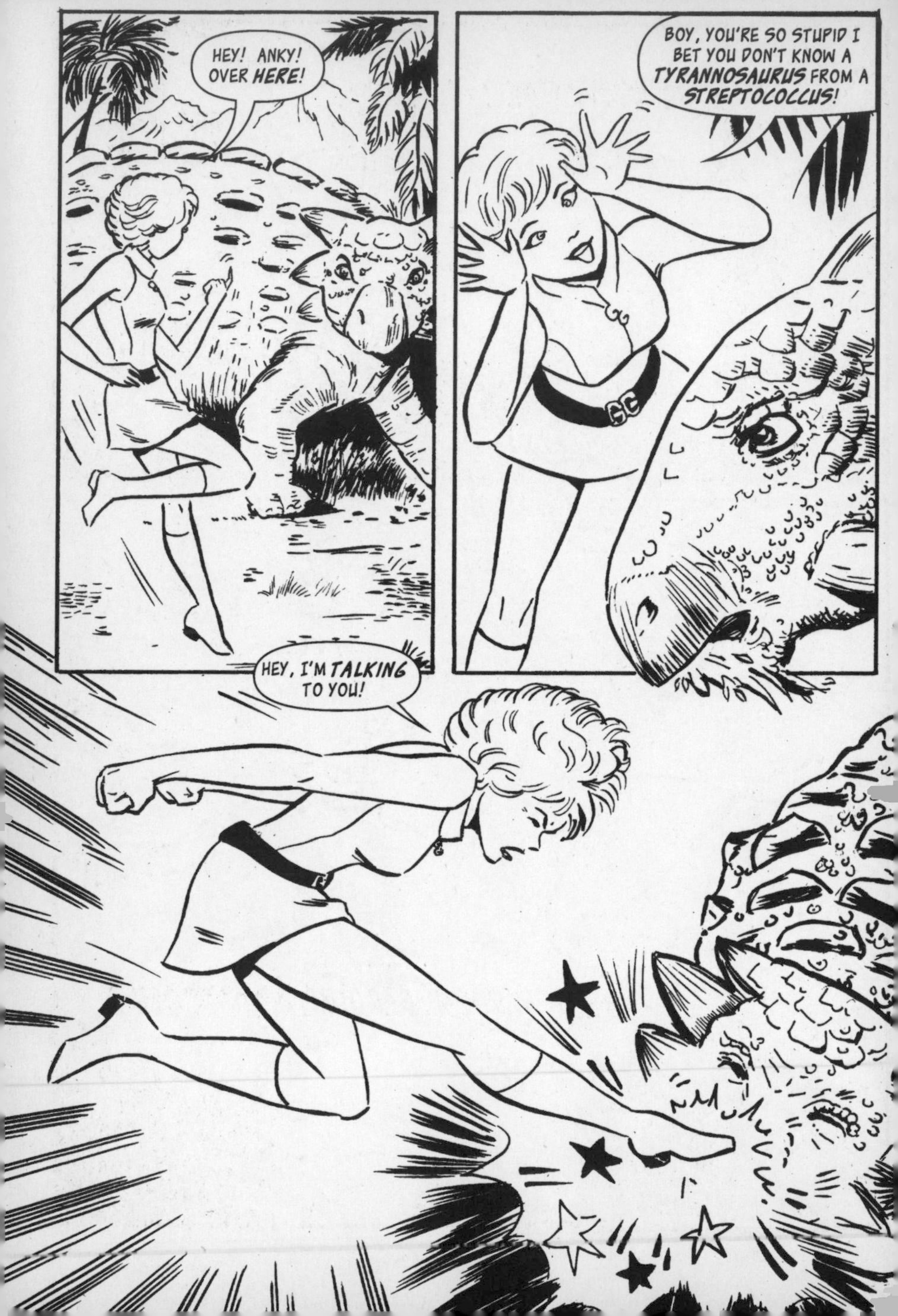
HEY! ANKY! OVER HERE!
BOY, YOU'RE SO STUPID I BET YOU DON'T KNOW A TYRANNOSAURUS FROM A STREPTOCOCCUS!
HEY, I'M TALKING TO YOU!

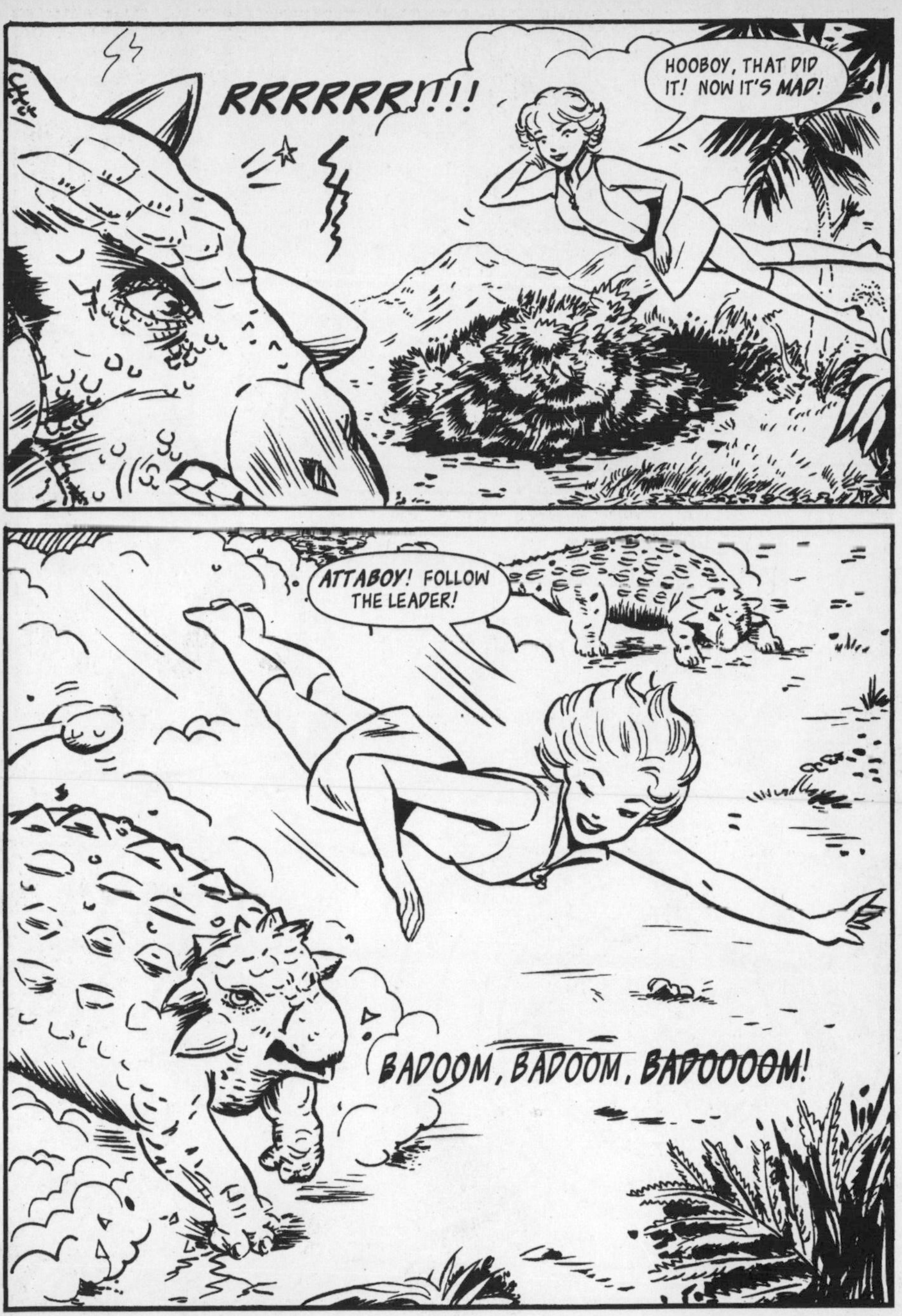
RRRRRR!!!!
HOOBOY, THAT DID IT! NOW IT'S MAD!
ATTABOY! FOLLOW THE LEADER!
BADOOM, BADOOM, BADOOOOM!

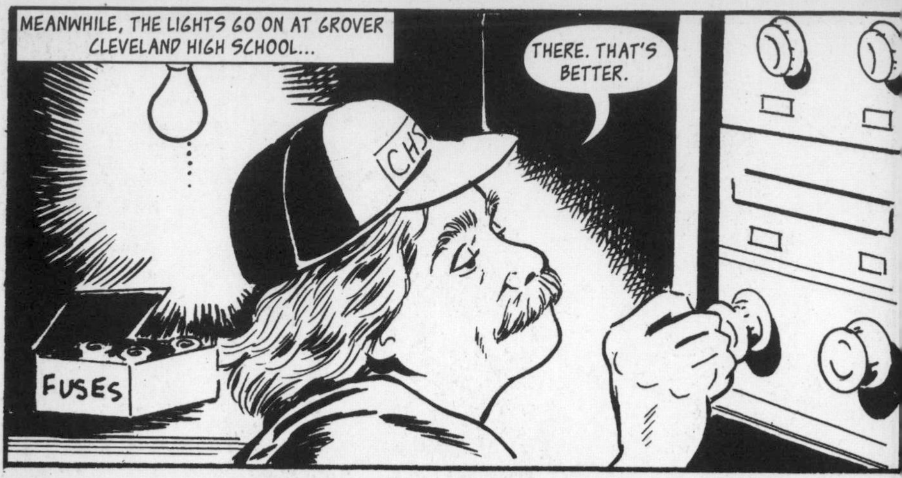
MEANWHILE, THE LIGHTS GO ON AT GROVER CLEVELAND HIGH SCHOOL...
THERE. THAT'S BETTER.
CHS
FUSES

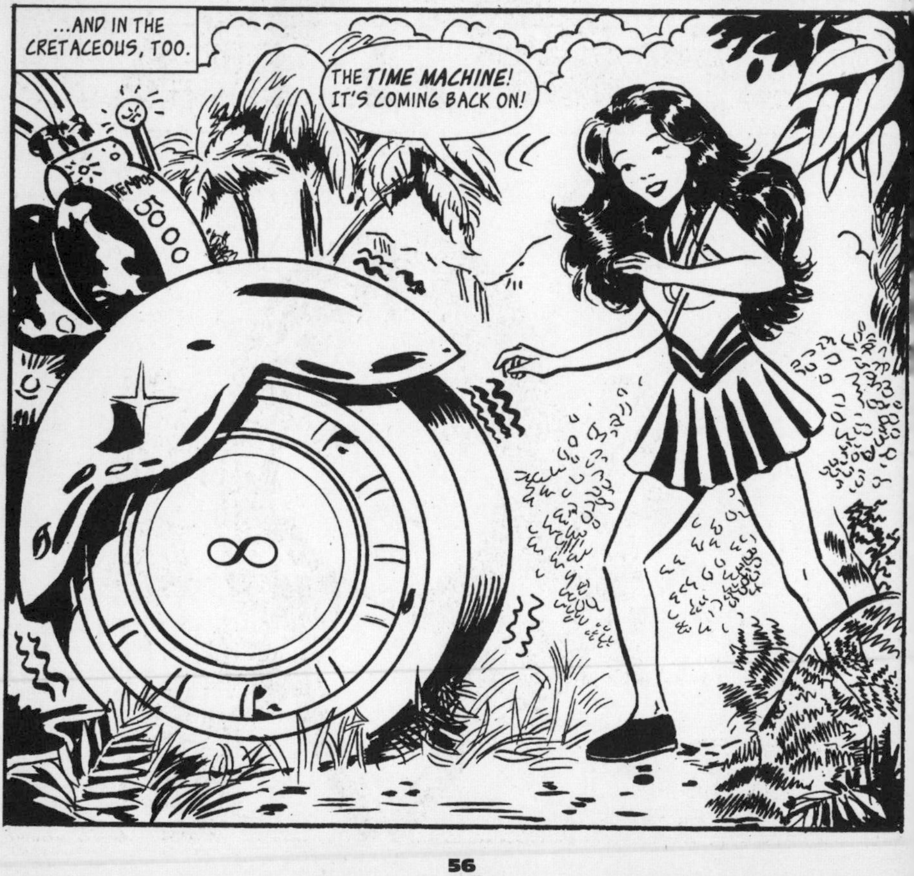
...AND IN THE CRETACEOUS, TOO.
THE *TIME MACHINE!* IT'S COMING BACK ON!
TEMPUS
5000

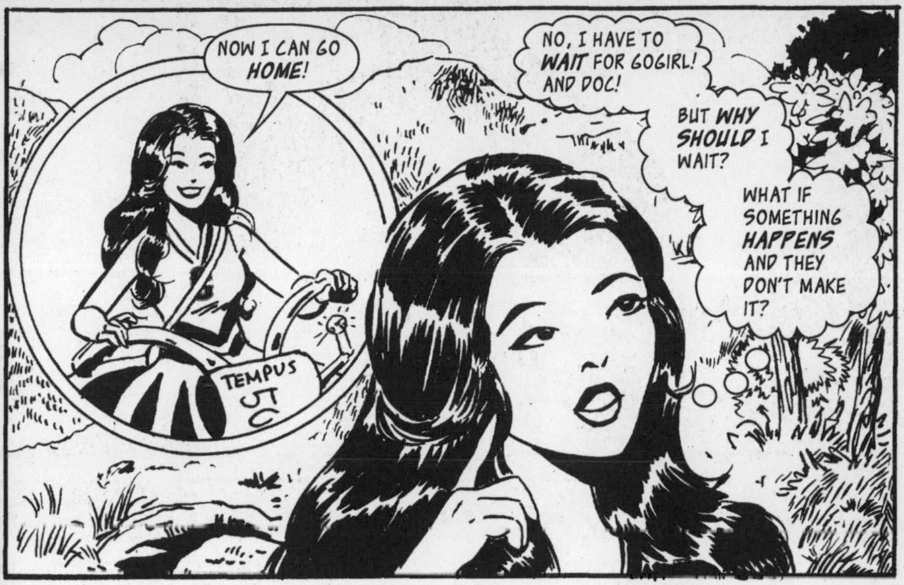
NOW I CAN GO HOME!
NO, I HAVE TO WAIT FOR GOGIRL! AND DOC!
BUT WHY SHOULD I WAIT?
WHAT IF SOMETHING HAPPENS AND THEY DON'T MAKE IT?
TEMPUS

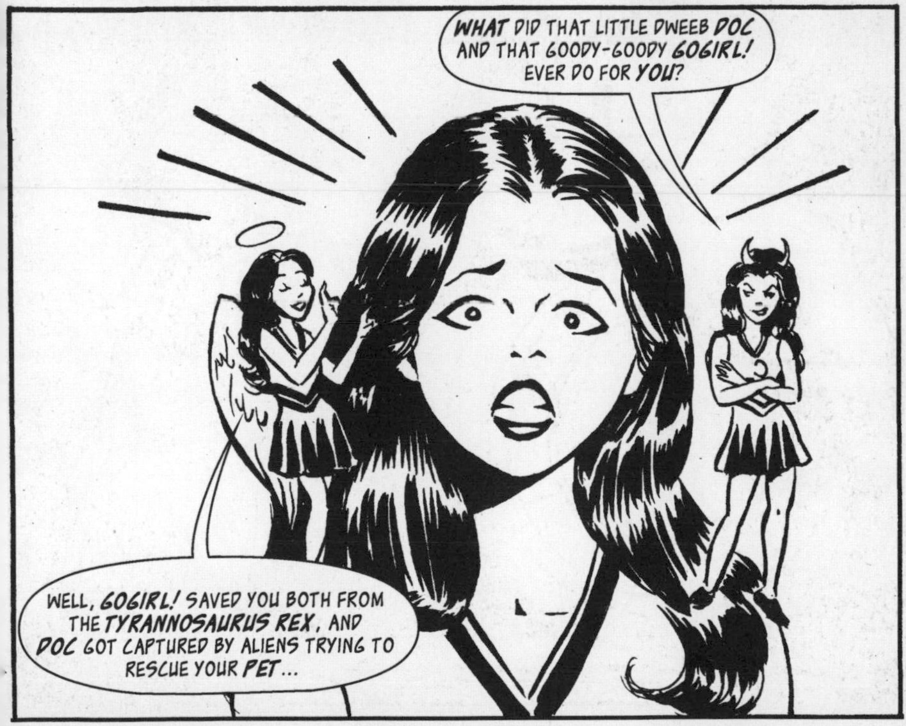
WHAT DID THAT LITTLE DWEEB DOC AND THAT GOODY-GOODY GOGIRL! EVER DO FOR YOU?
WELL, GOGIRL! SAVED YOU BOTH FROM THE TYRANNOSAURUS REX, AND DOC GOT CAPTURED BY ALIENS TRYING TO RESCUE YOUR PET...

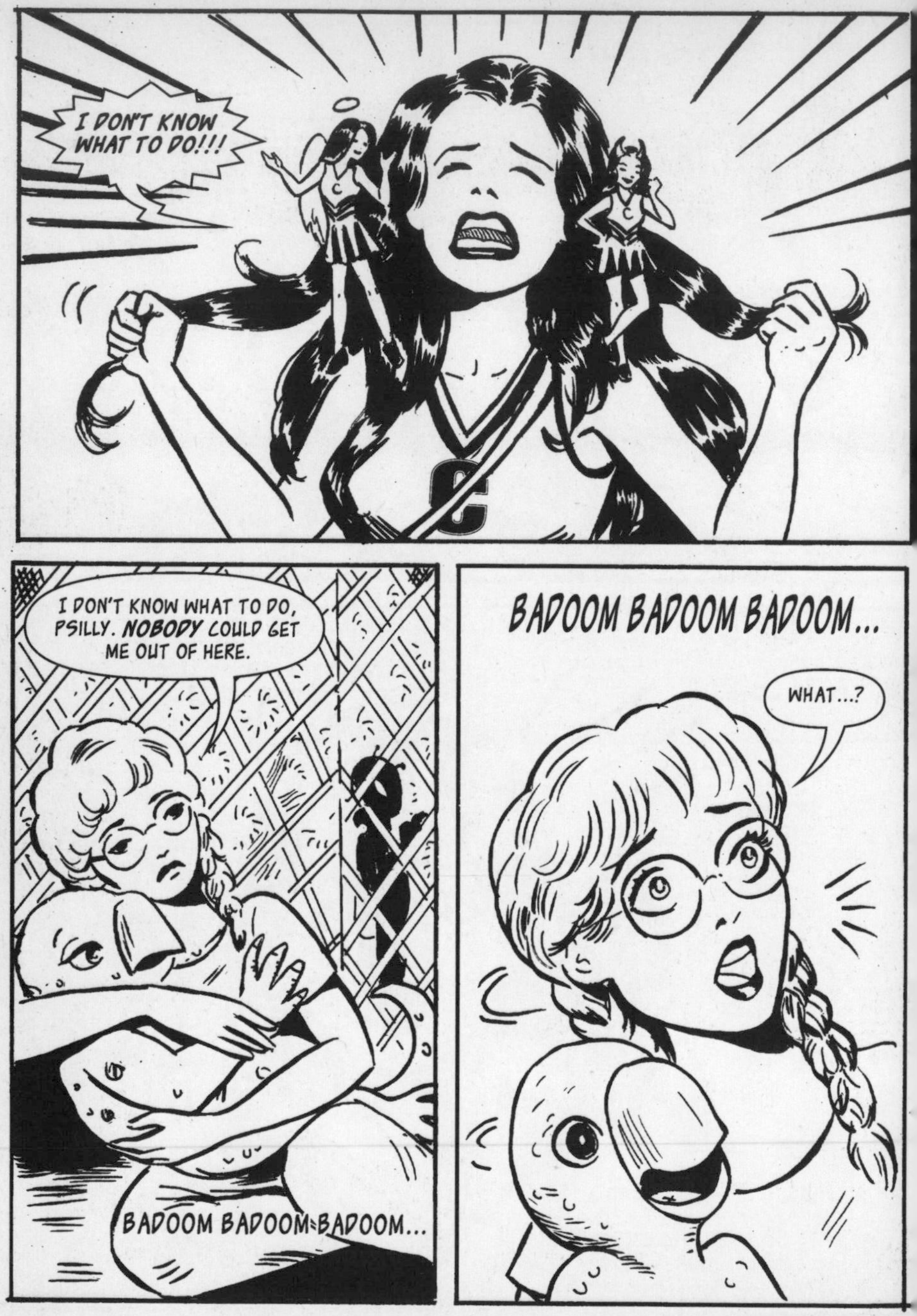
I DON'T KNOW WHAT TO DO!!!
I DON'T KNOW WHAT TO DO, PSILLY. NOBODY COULD GET ME OUT OF HERE.
BADOOM BADOOM BADOOM...
BADOOM BADOOM BADOOM...
WHAT...?

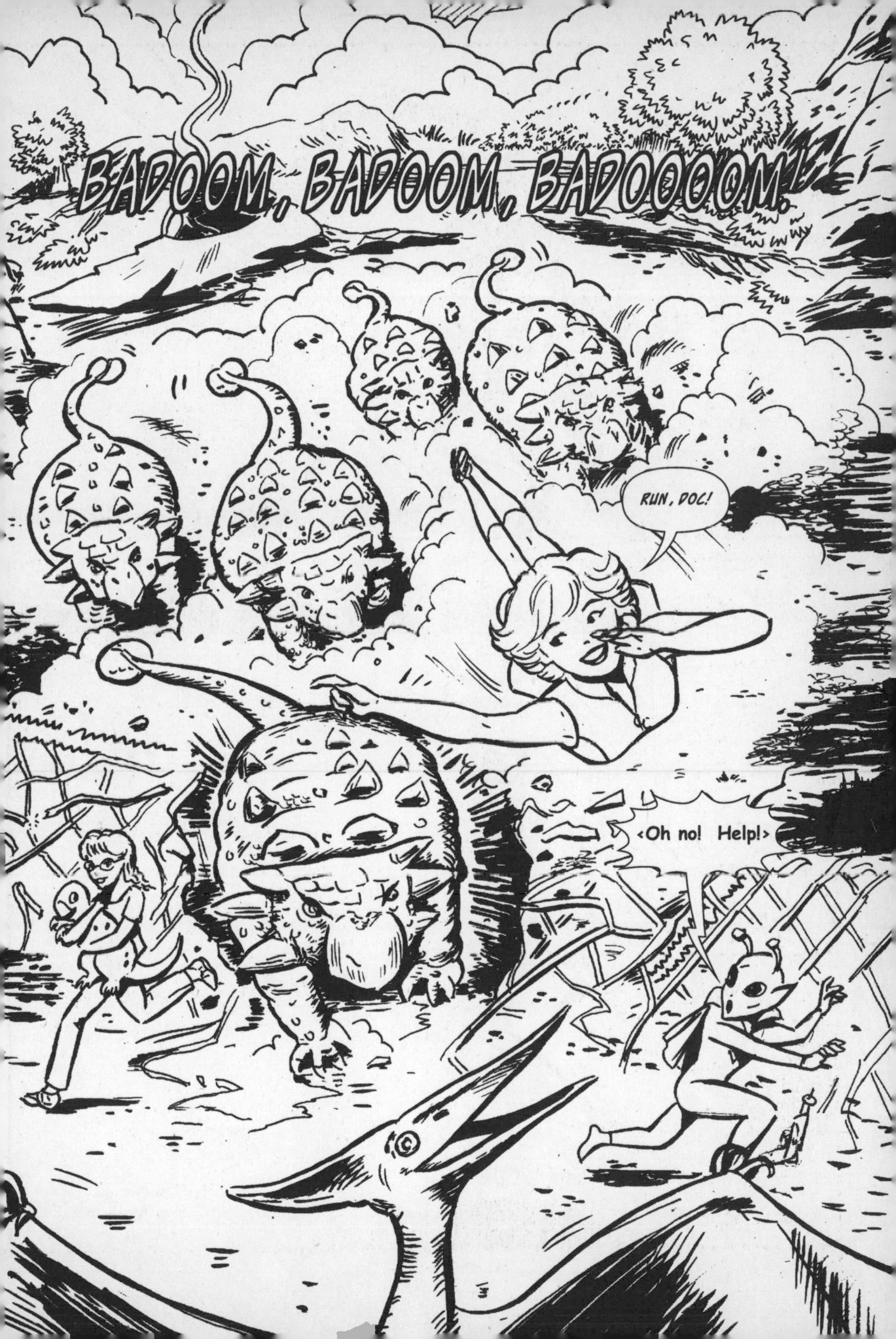
BADOOM, BADOOM, BADOOOOM!
RUN, DOC!
<Oh no! Help!>

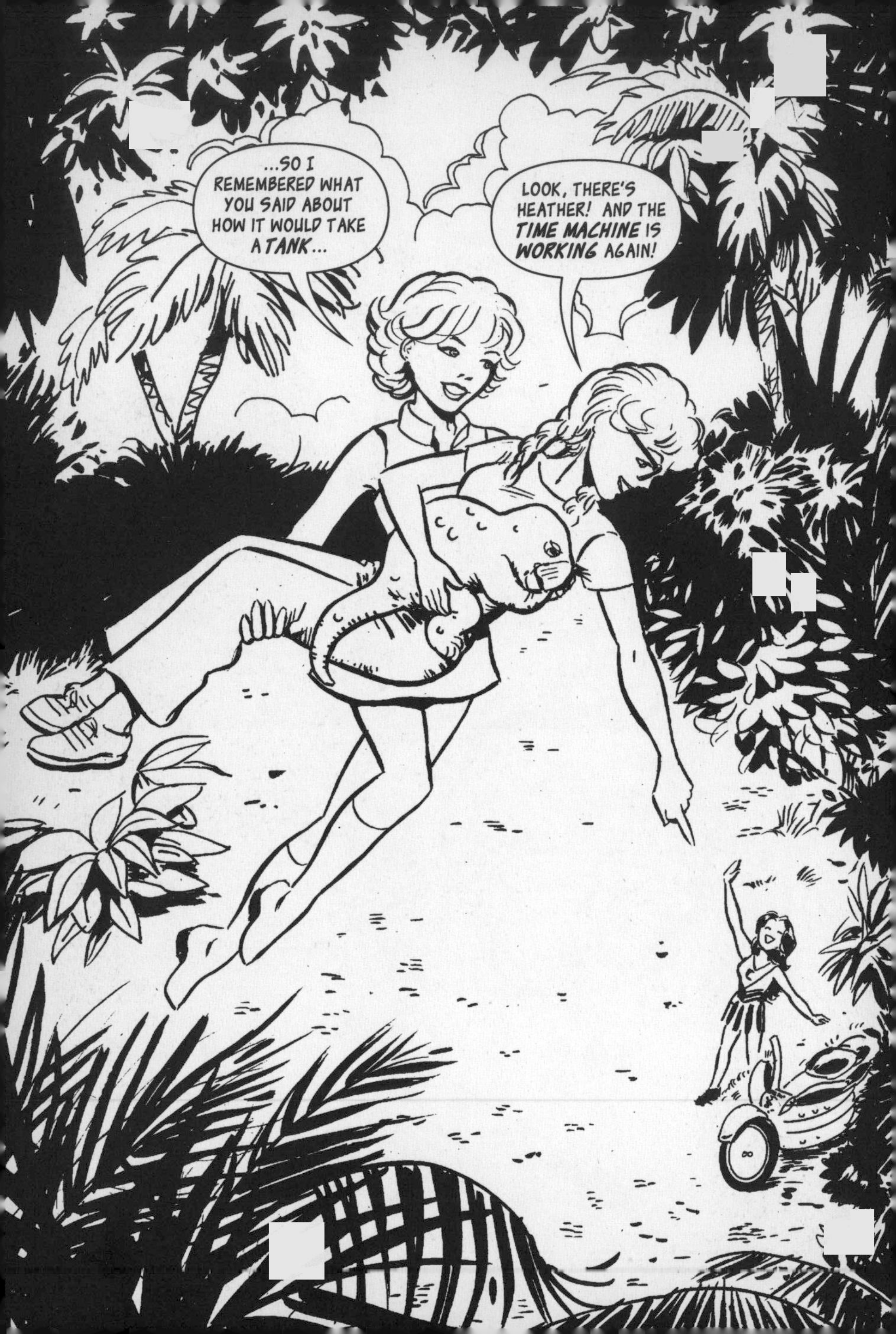
...SO I REMEMBERED WHAT YOU SAID ABOUT HOW IT WOULD TAKE A TANK...
LOOK, THERE'S HEATHER! AND THE TIME MACHINE IS WORKING AGAIN!

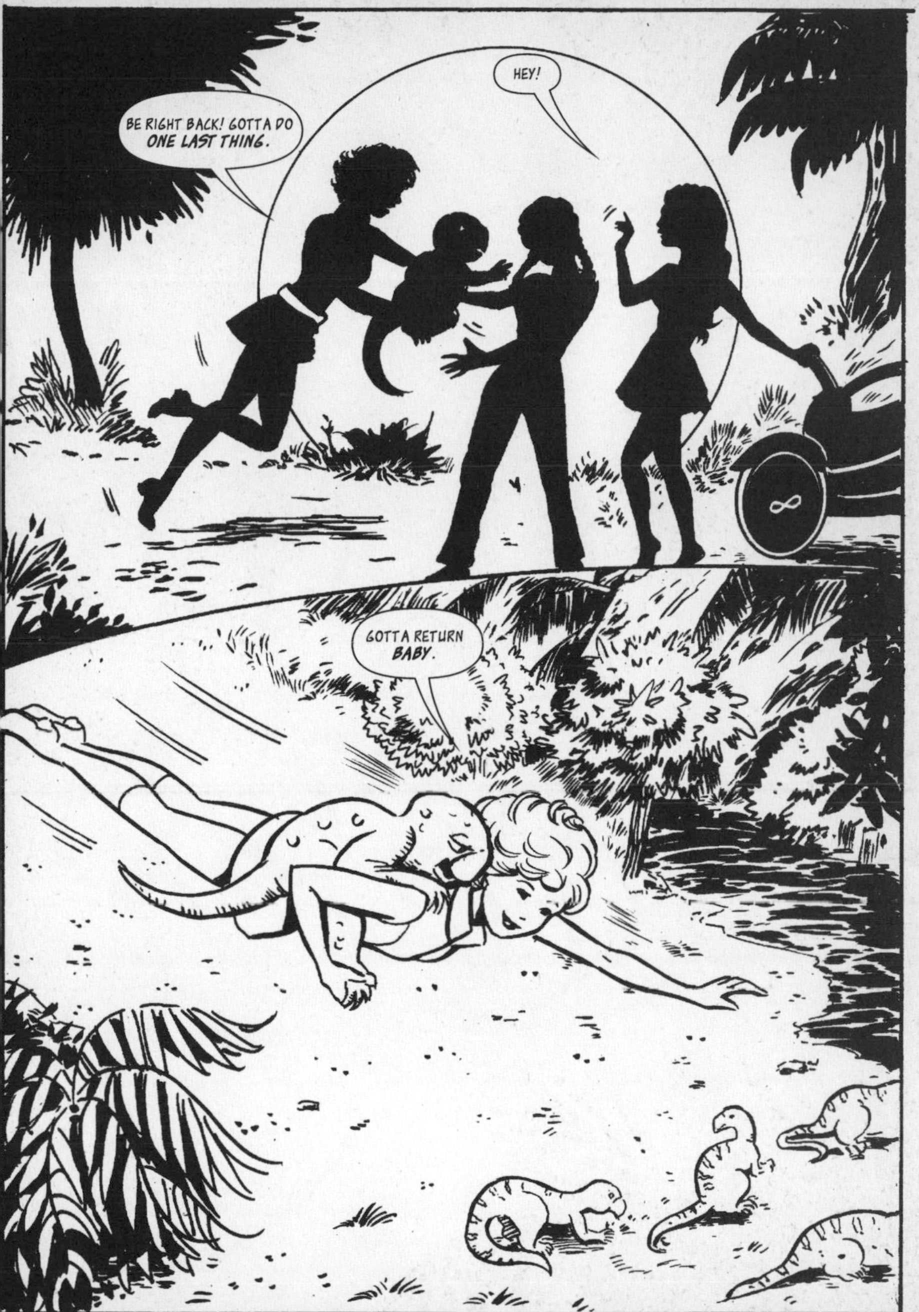
BE RIGHT BACK! GOTTA DO ONE LAST THING.
HEY!
GOTTA RETURN BABY.

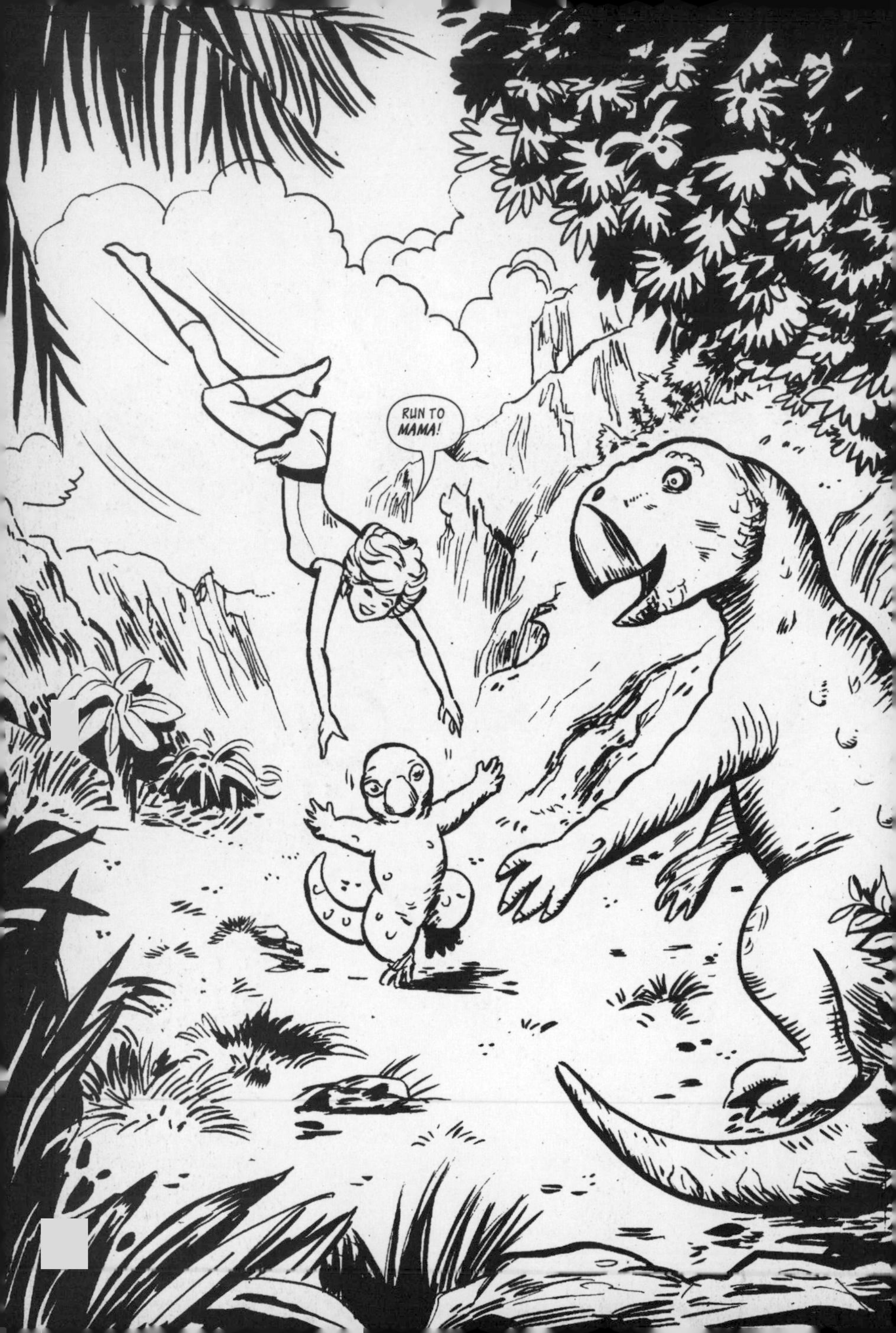
RUN TO MAMA!

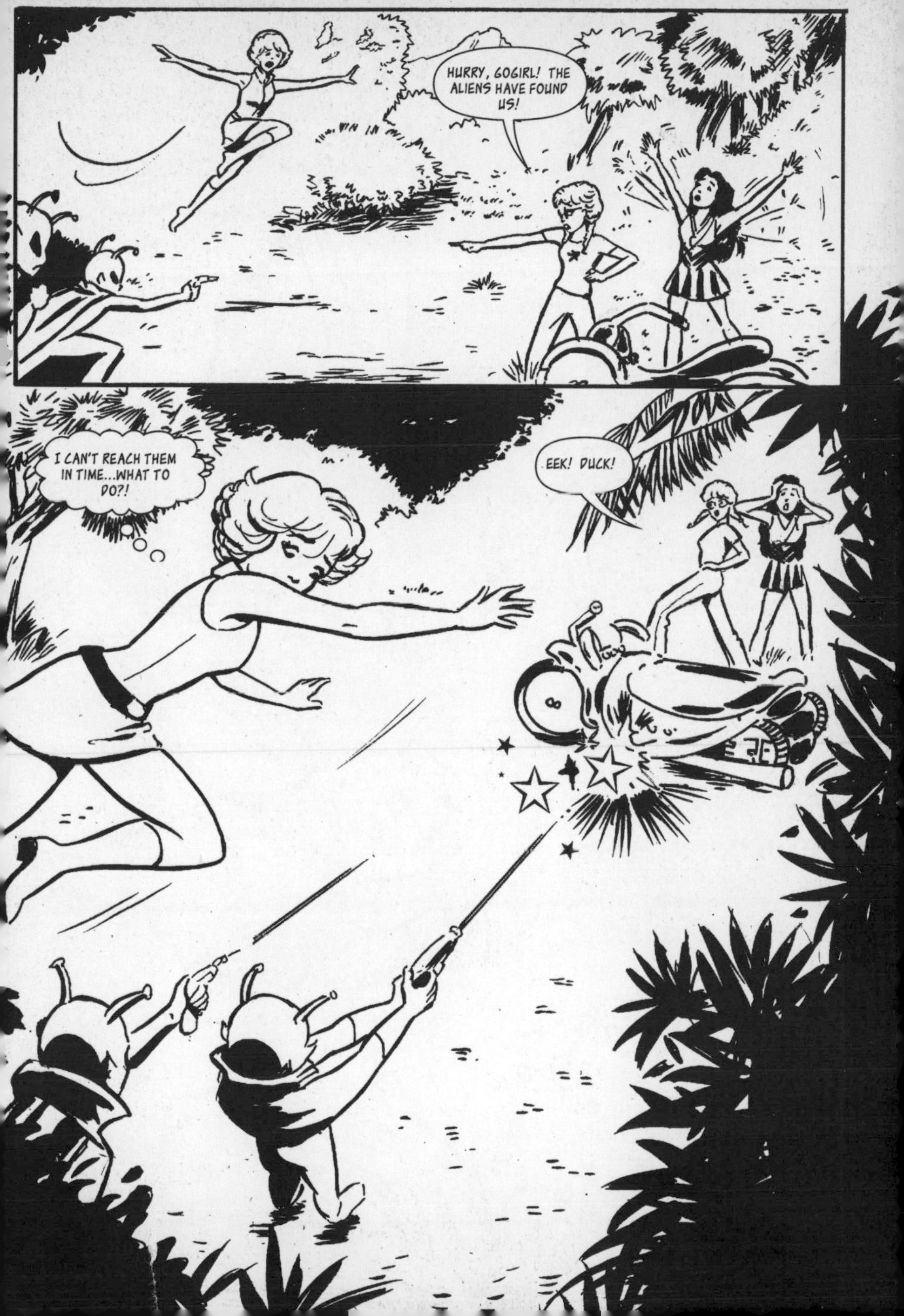
HURRY, GOGIRL! THE ALIENS HAVE FOUND US!
I CAN'T REACH THEM IN TIME...WHAT TO DO?!
EEK! DUCK!

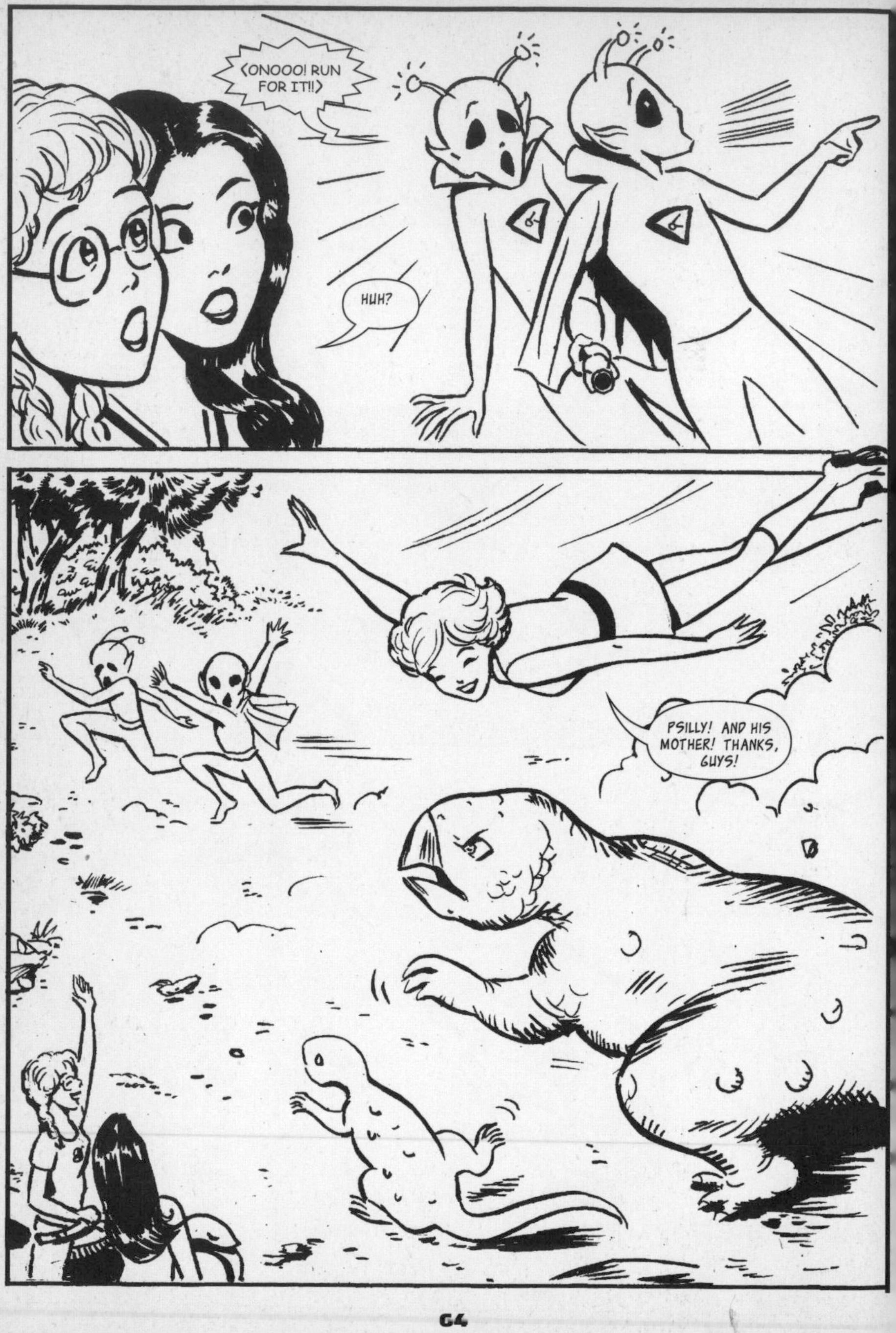
‹ONOOO! RUN FOR IT!!›
HUH?
PSILLY! AND HIS MOTHER! THANKS, GUYS!

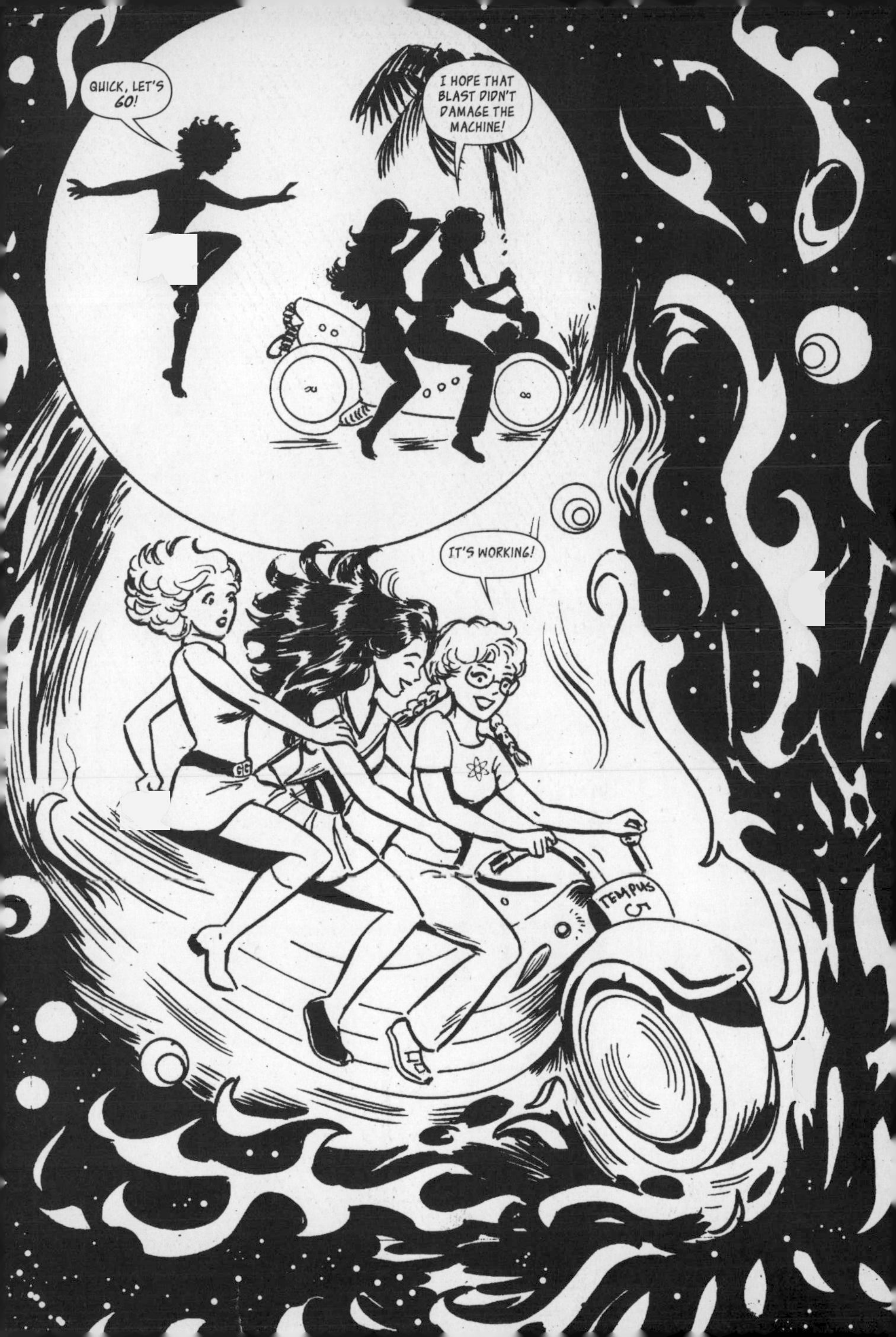
QUICK, LET'S GO!
I HOPE THAT BLAST DIDN'T DAMAGE THE MACHINE!
IT'S WORKING!
TEMPUS 5

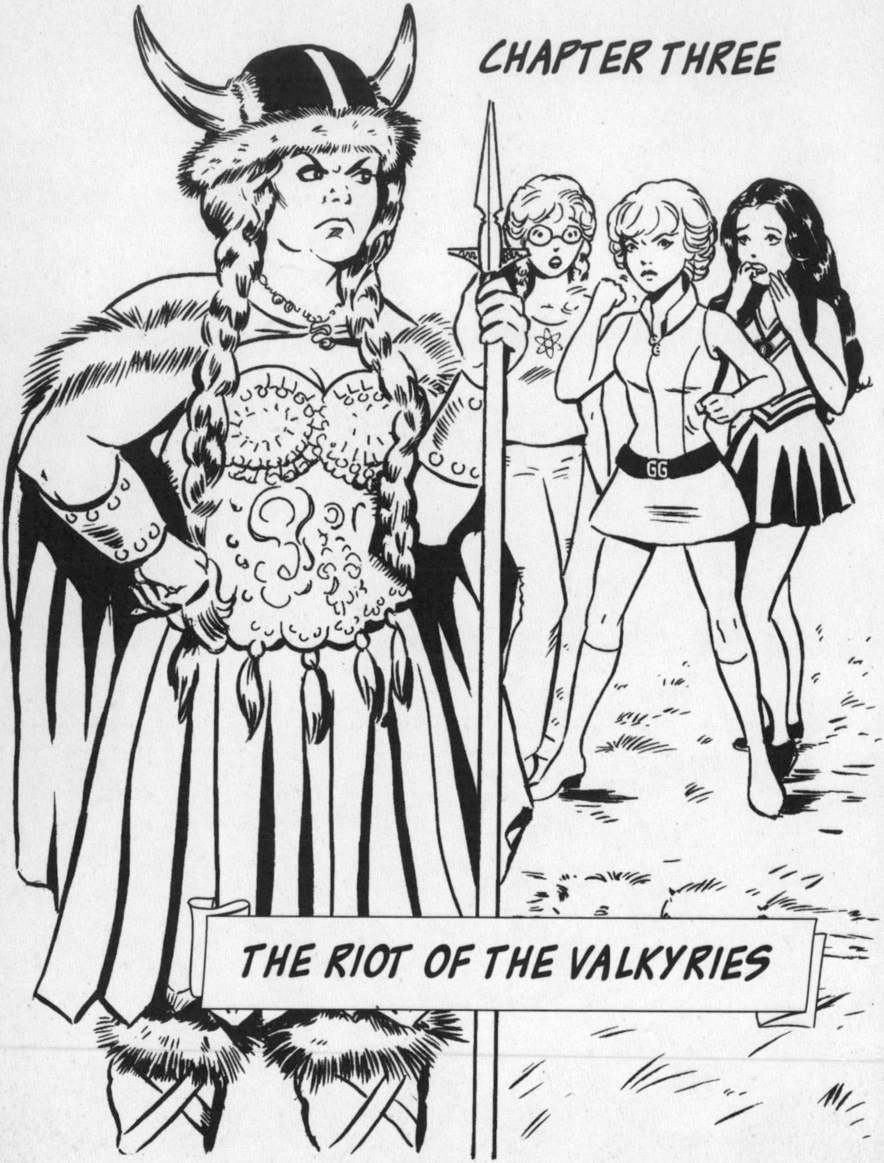
CHAPTER THREE
THE RIOT OF THE VALKYRIES

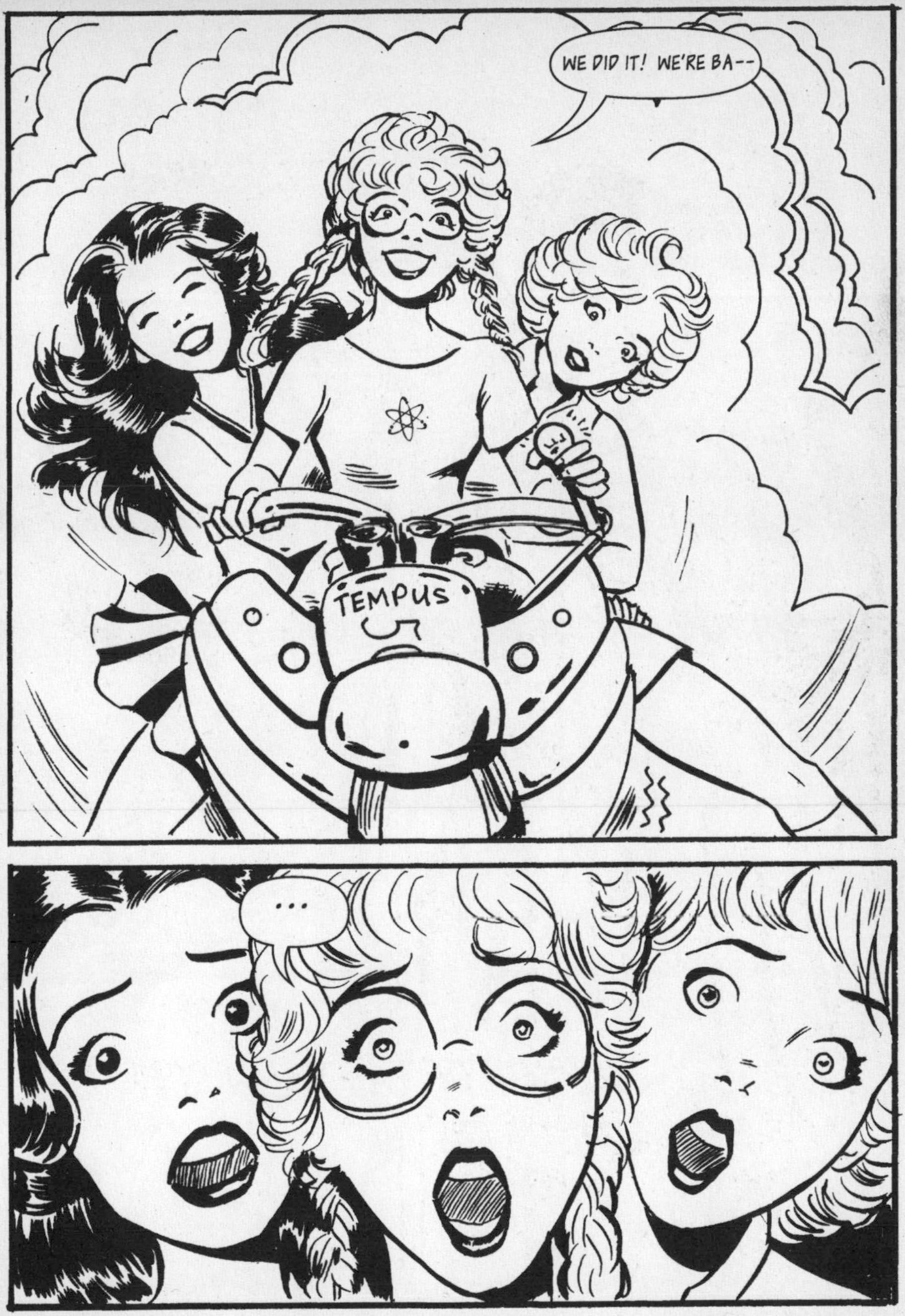
WE DID IT! WE'RE BA--
TEMPUS
...

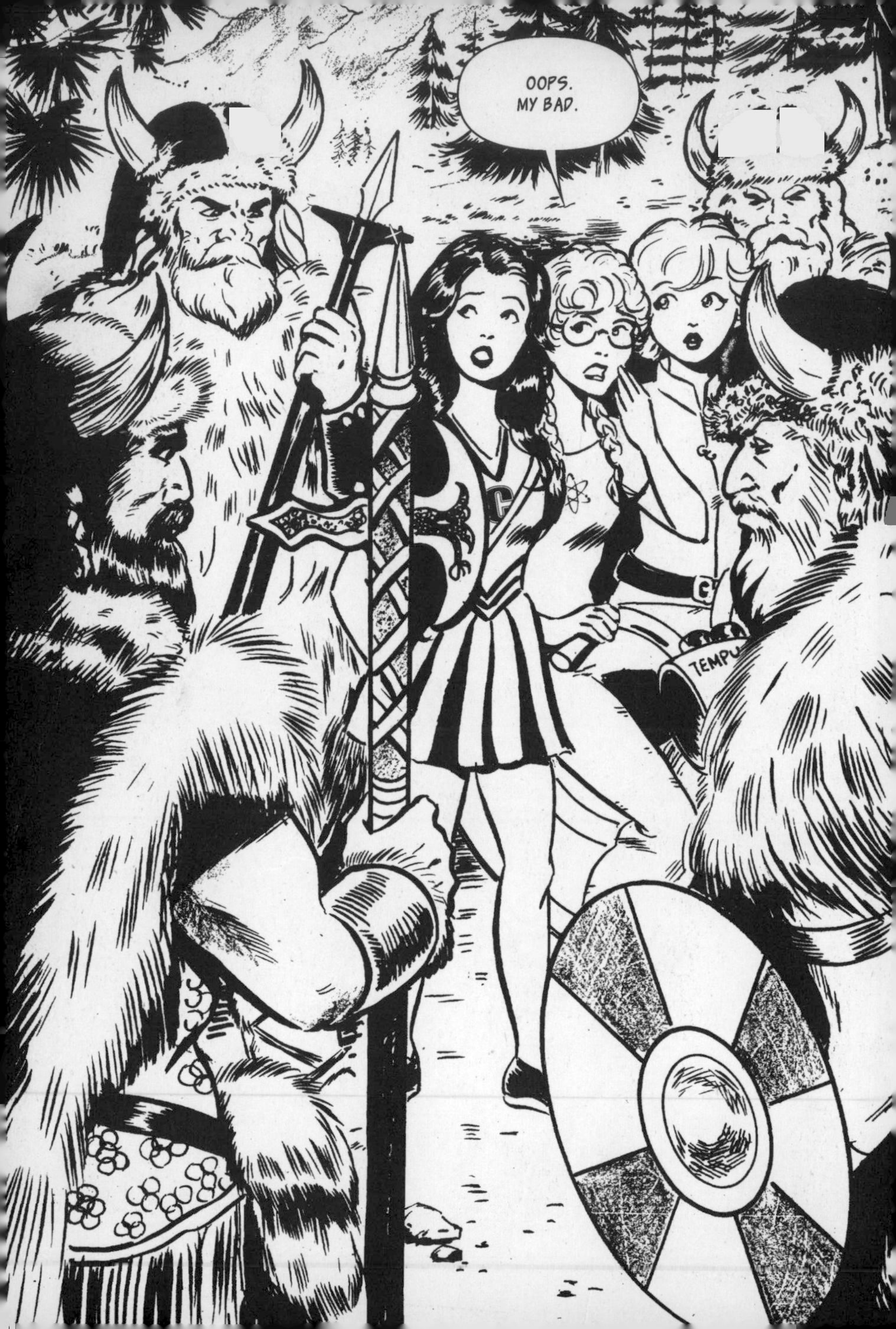
OOPS.
MY BAD.
TEMPU

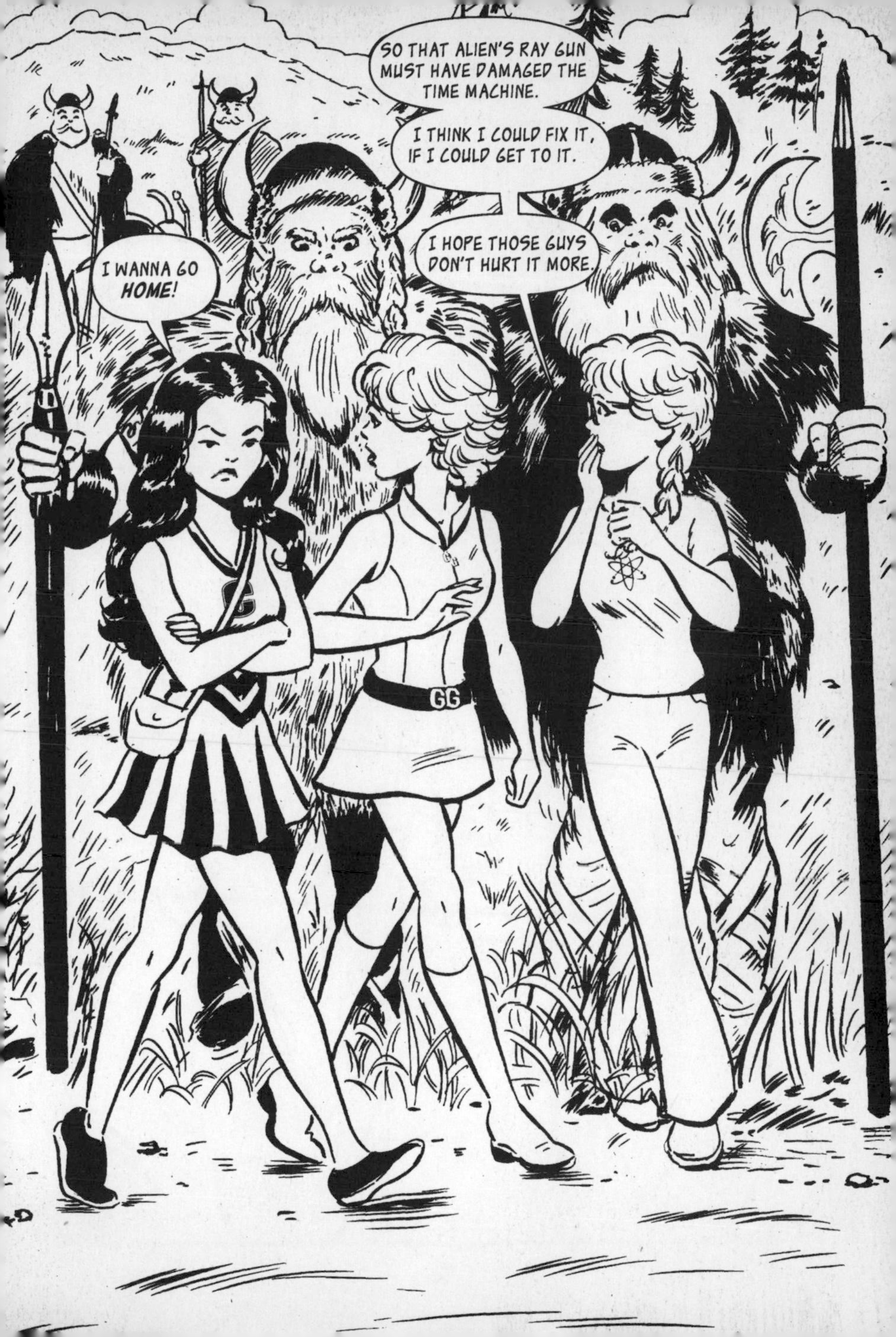
I WANNA GO HOME!
SO THAT ALIEN'S RAY GUN MUST HAVE DAMAGED THE TIME MACHINE.
I THINK I COULD FIX IT, IF I COULD GET TO IT.
I HOPE THOSE GUYS DON'T HURT IT MORE.

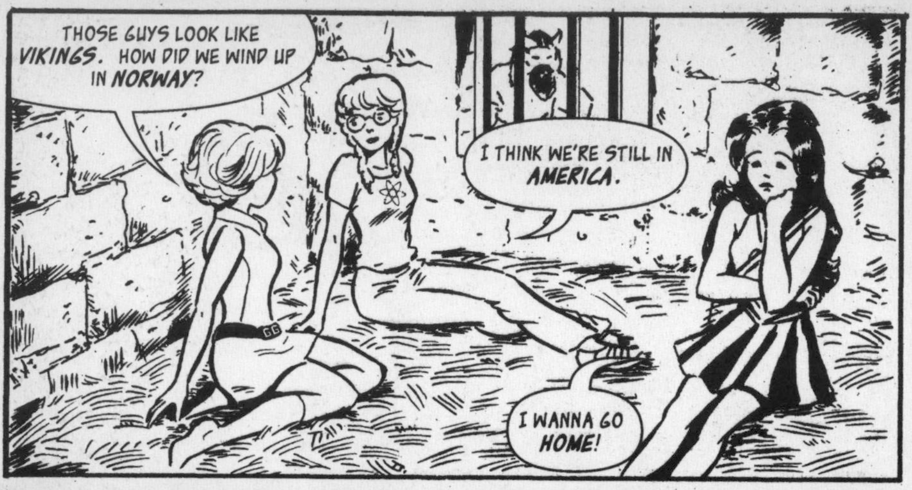
THOSE GUYS LOOK LIKE VIKINGS. HOW DID WE WIND UP IN NORWAY?
I THINK WE'RE STILL IN AMERICA.
I WANNA GO HOME!

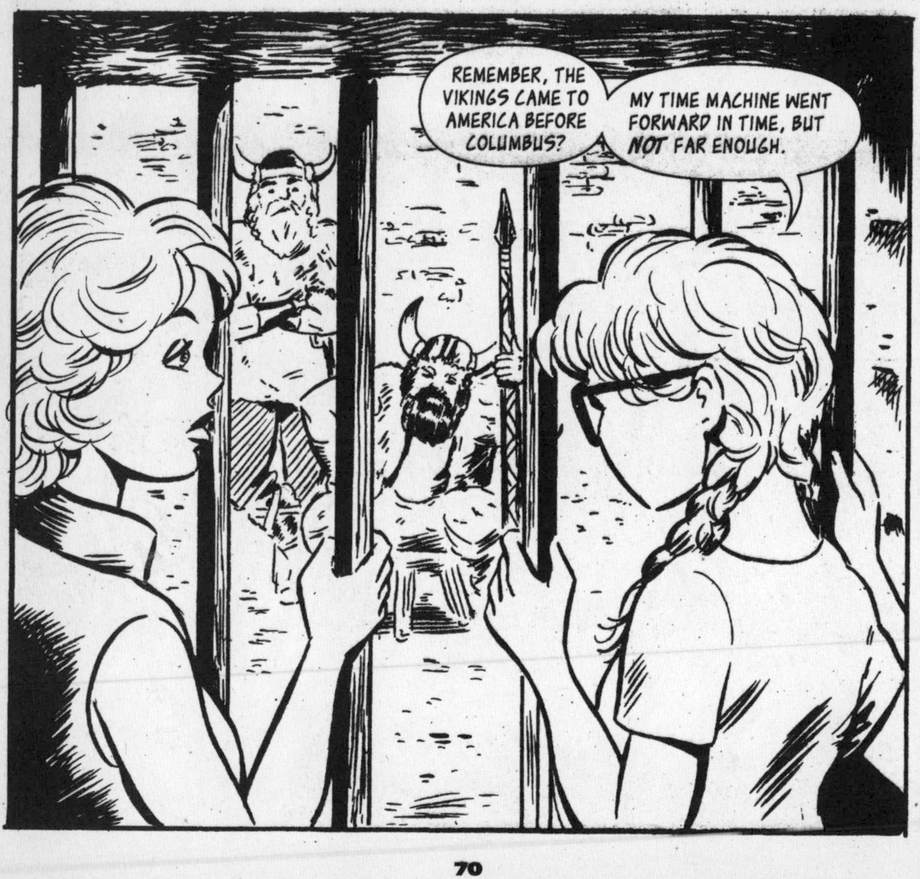
REMEMBER, THE VIKINGS CAME TO AMERICA BEFORE COLUMBUS?
MY TIME MACHINE WENT FORWARD IN TIME, BUT NOT FAR ENOUGH.

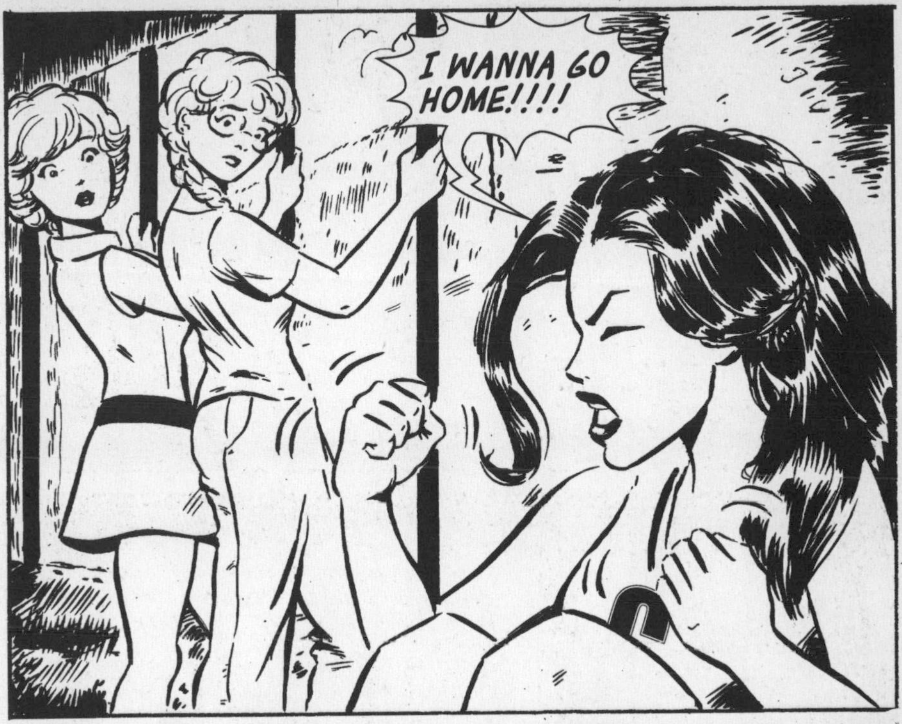
I WANNA GO HOME!!!!

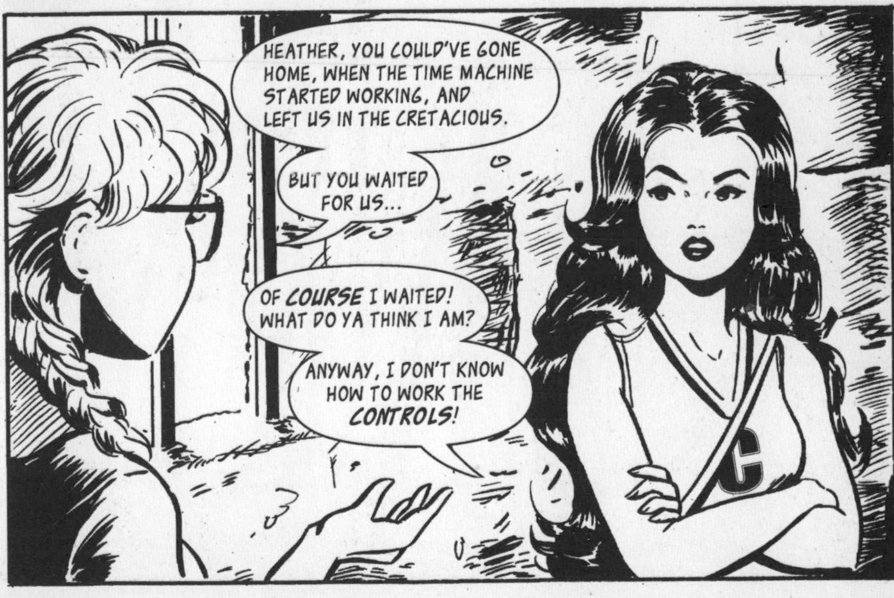
HEATHER, YOU COULD'VE GONE HOME, WHEN THE TIME MACHINE STARTED WORKING, AND LEFT US IN THE CRETACIOUS.
BUT YOU WAITED FOR US...
OF COURSE I WAITED! WHAT DO YA THINK I AM?
ANYWAY, I DON'T KNOW HOW TO WORK THE CONTROLS!

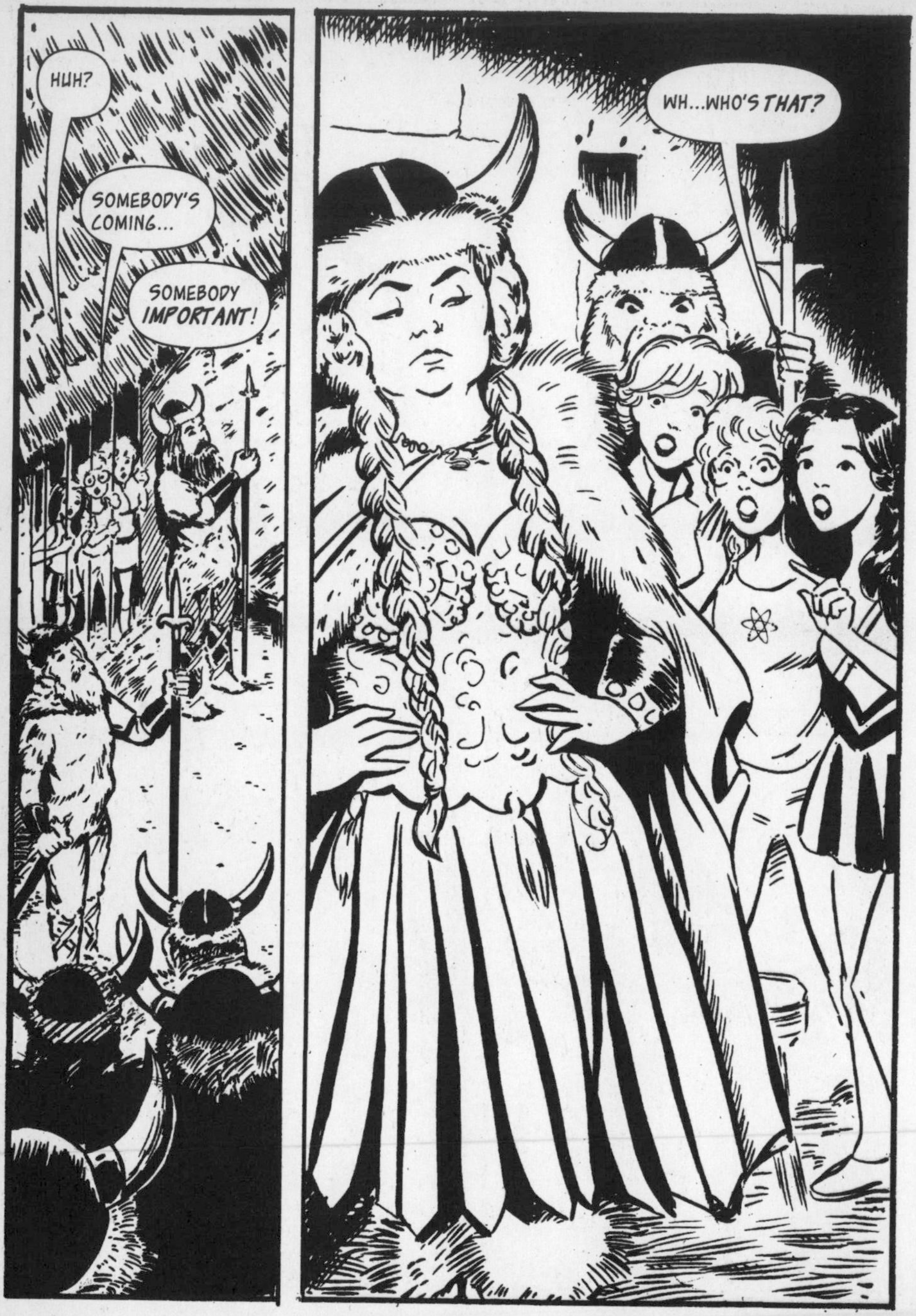
HUH?
SOMEBODY'S COMING...
SOMEBODY IMPORTANT!
WH...WHO'S THAT?

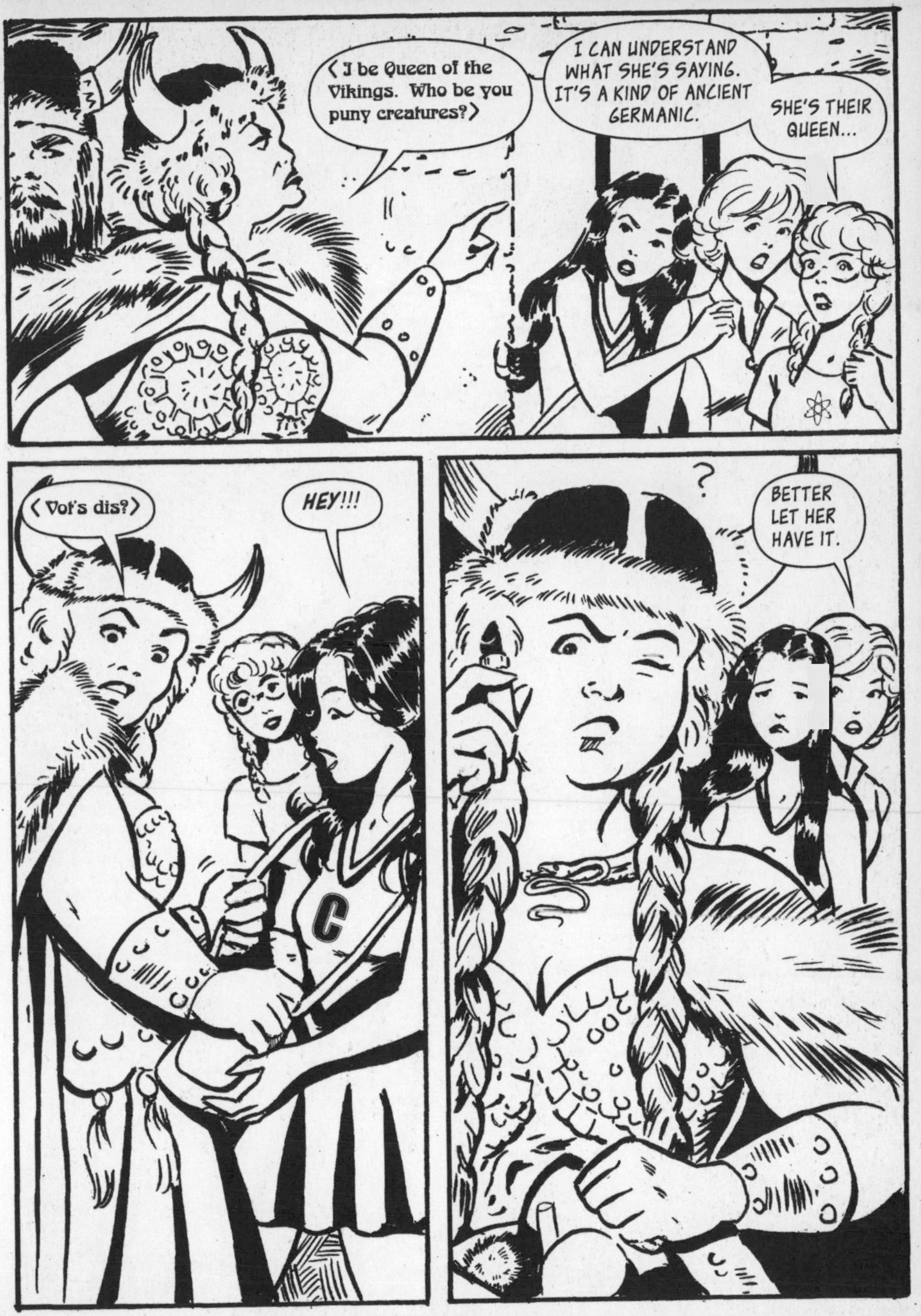

〈 I be Queen of the Vikings. Who be you puny creatures?〉
I CAN UNDERSTAND WHAT SHE'S SAYING. IT'S A KIND OF ANCIENT GERMANIC.
SHE'S THEIR QUEEN...
〈 Vot's dis?〉
HEY!!!
?
BETTER LET HER HAVE IT.

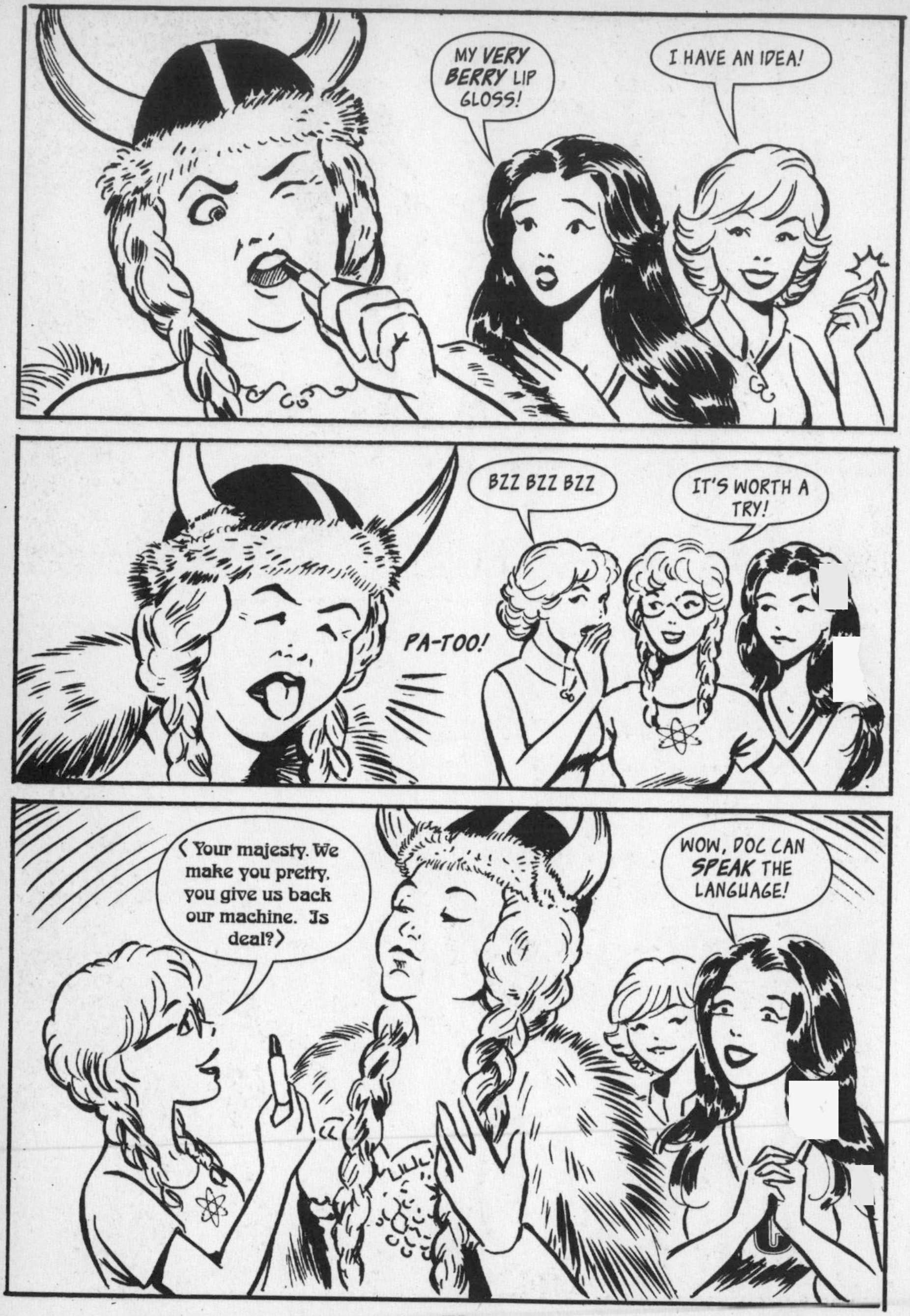
MY VERY BERRY LIP GLOSS!
I HAVE AN IDEA!
BZZ BZZ BZZ
IT'S WORTH A TRY!
PA-TOO!
‹Your majesty. We make you pretty, you give us back our machine. Is deal?›
WOW, DOC CAN SPEAK THE LANGUAGE!

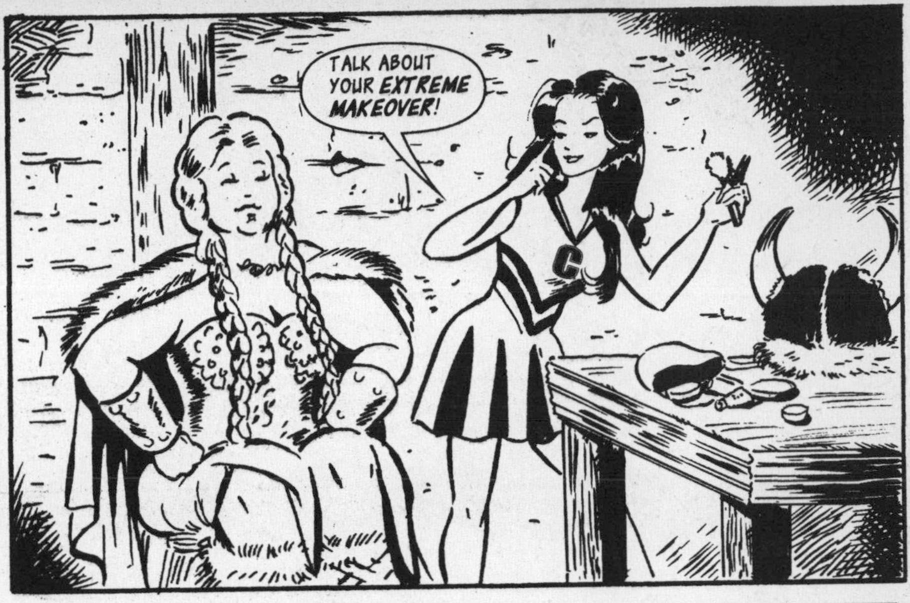
TALK ABOUT YOUR EXTREME MAKEOVER!

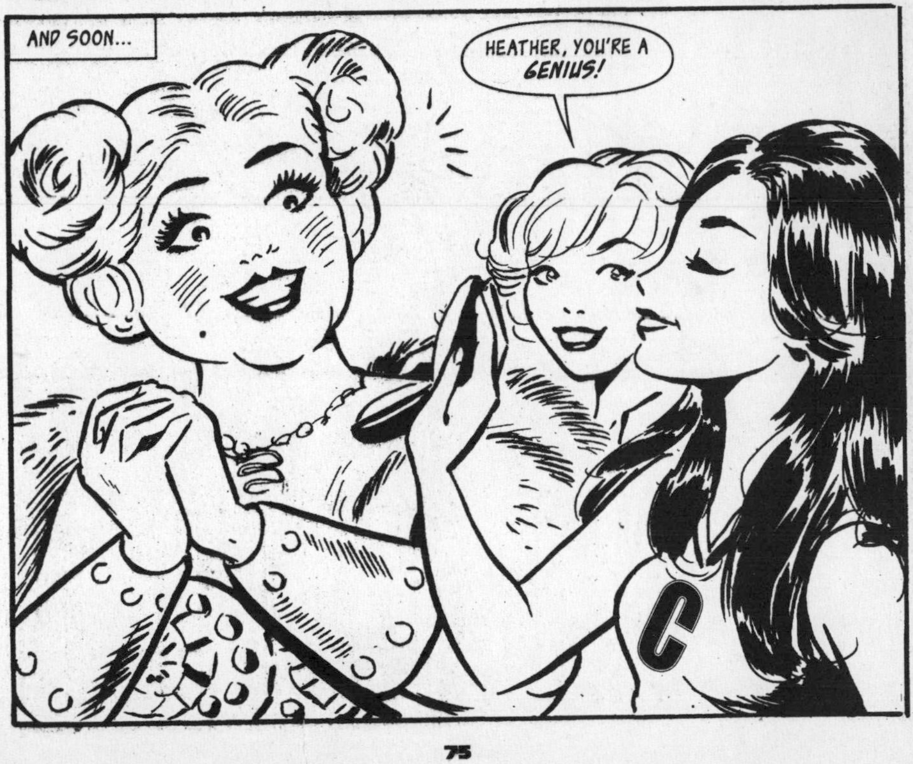
AND SOON...
HEATHER, YOU'RE A GENIUS!

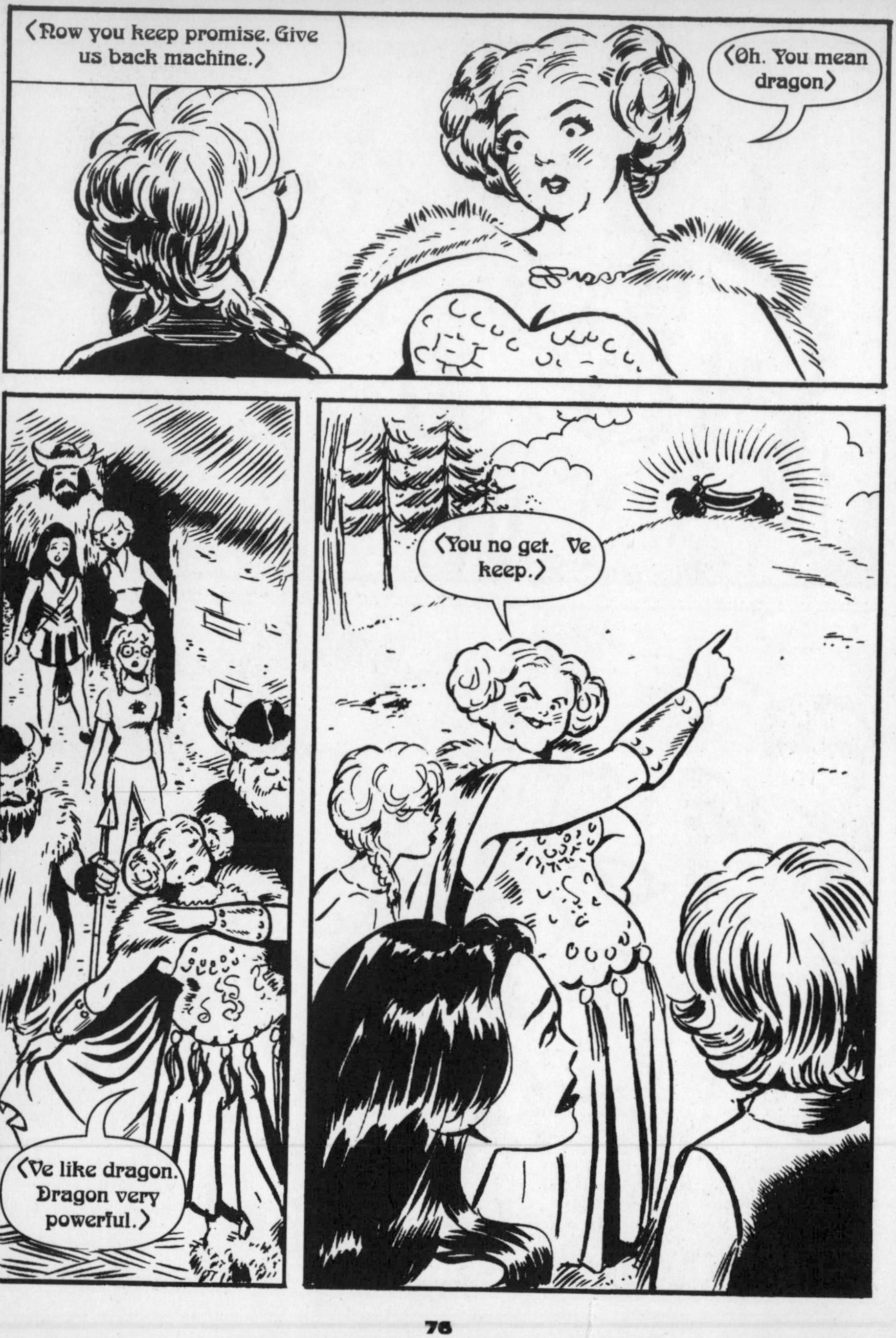

<Now you keep promise. Give us back machine.>
<Oh. You mean dragon>
<Ve like dragon. Dragon very powerful.>
<You no get. Ve keep.>

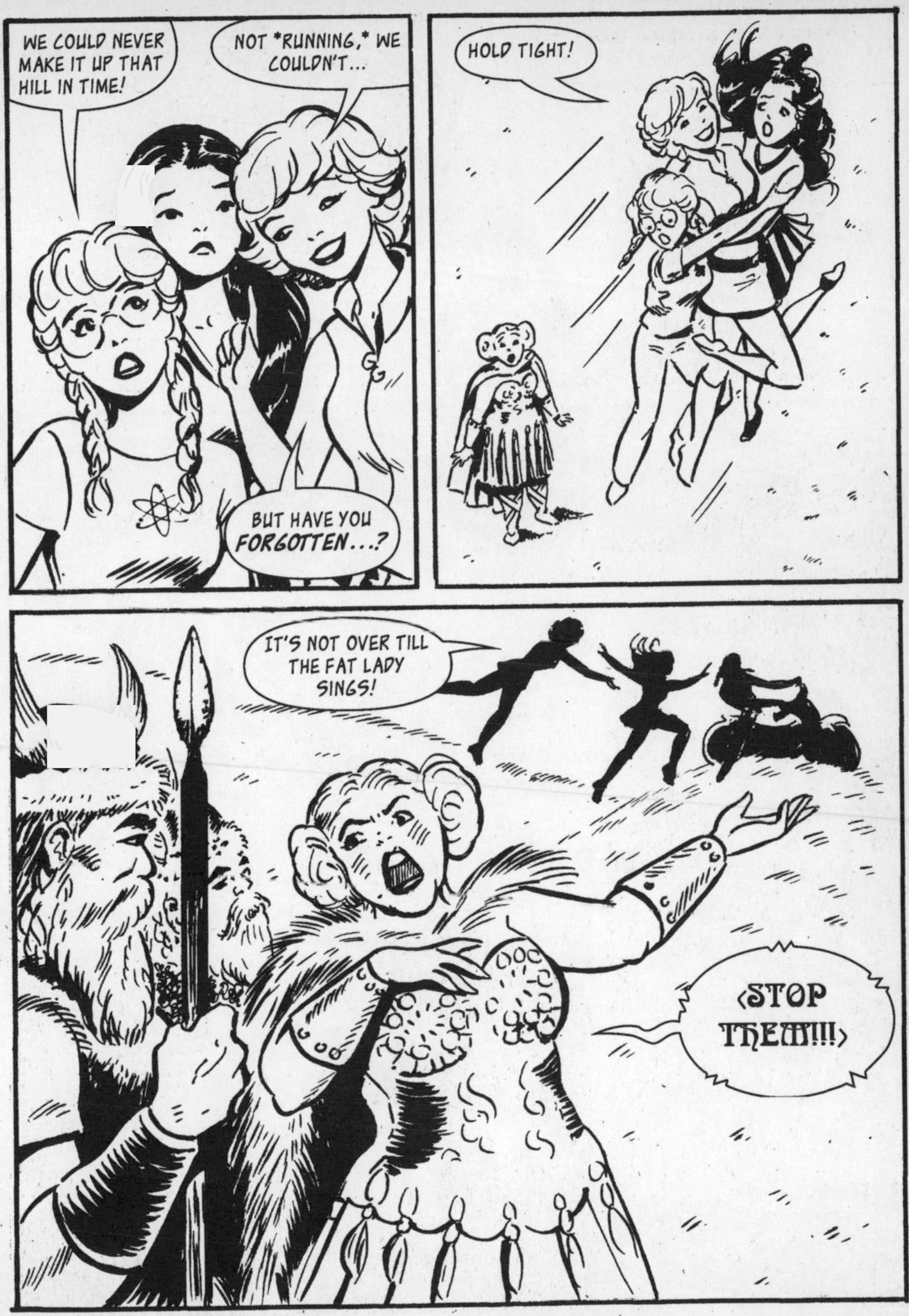
WE COULD NEVER MAKE IT UP THAT HILL IN TIME!
NOT *RUNNING,* WE COULDN'T...
BUT HAVE YOU FORGOTTEN...?
HOLD TIGHT!
IT'S NOT OVER TILL THE FAT LADY SINGS!
‹STOP THEM!!!›

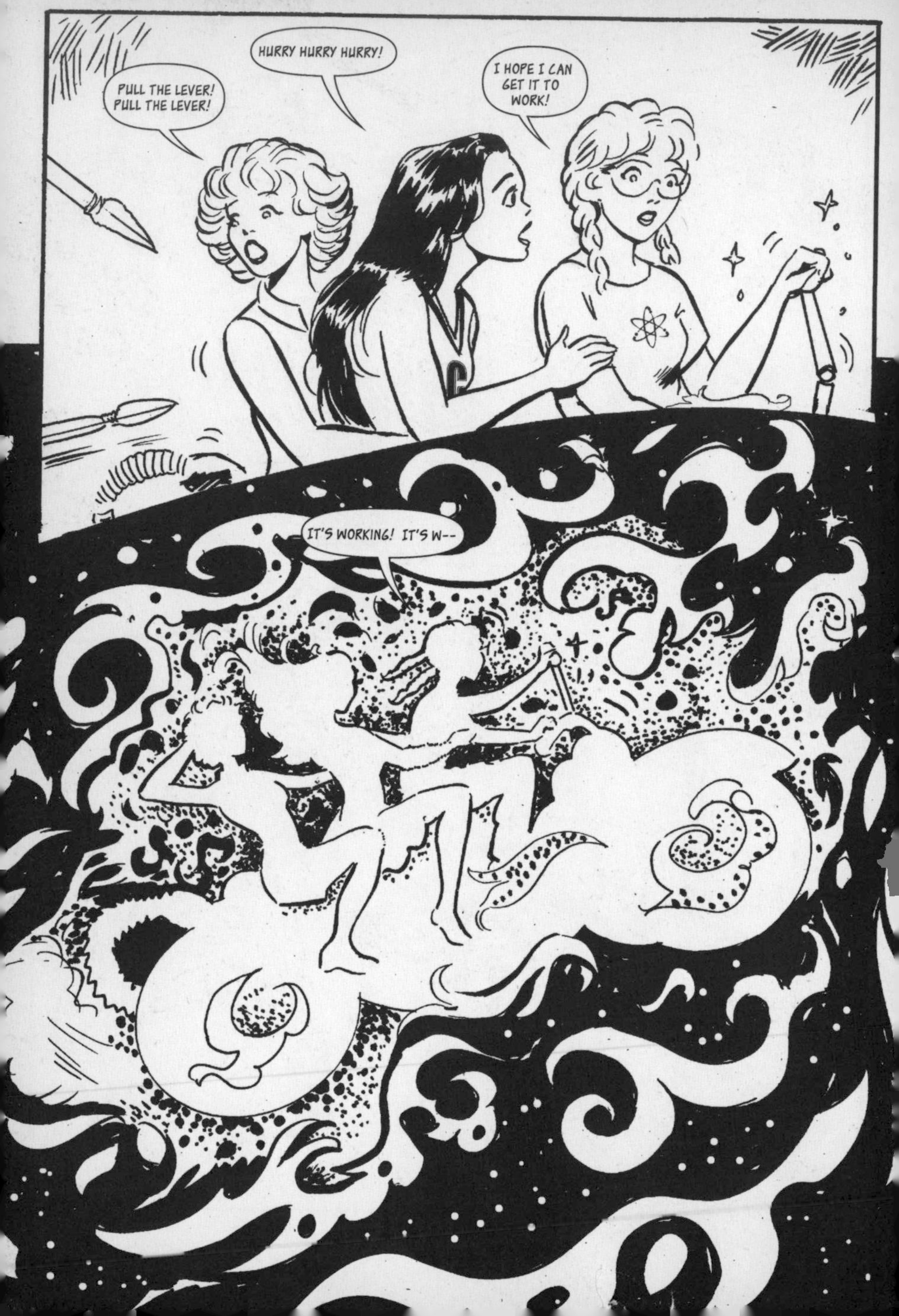
PULL THE LEVER! PULL THE LEVER!
HURRY HURRY HURRY!
I HOPE I CAN GET IT TO WORK!
IT'S WORKING! IT'S W--

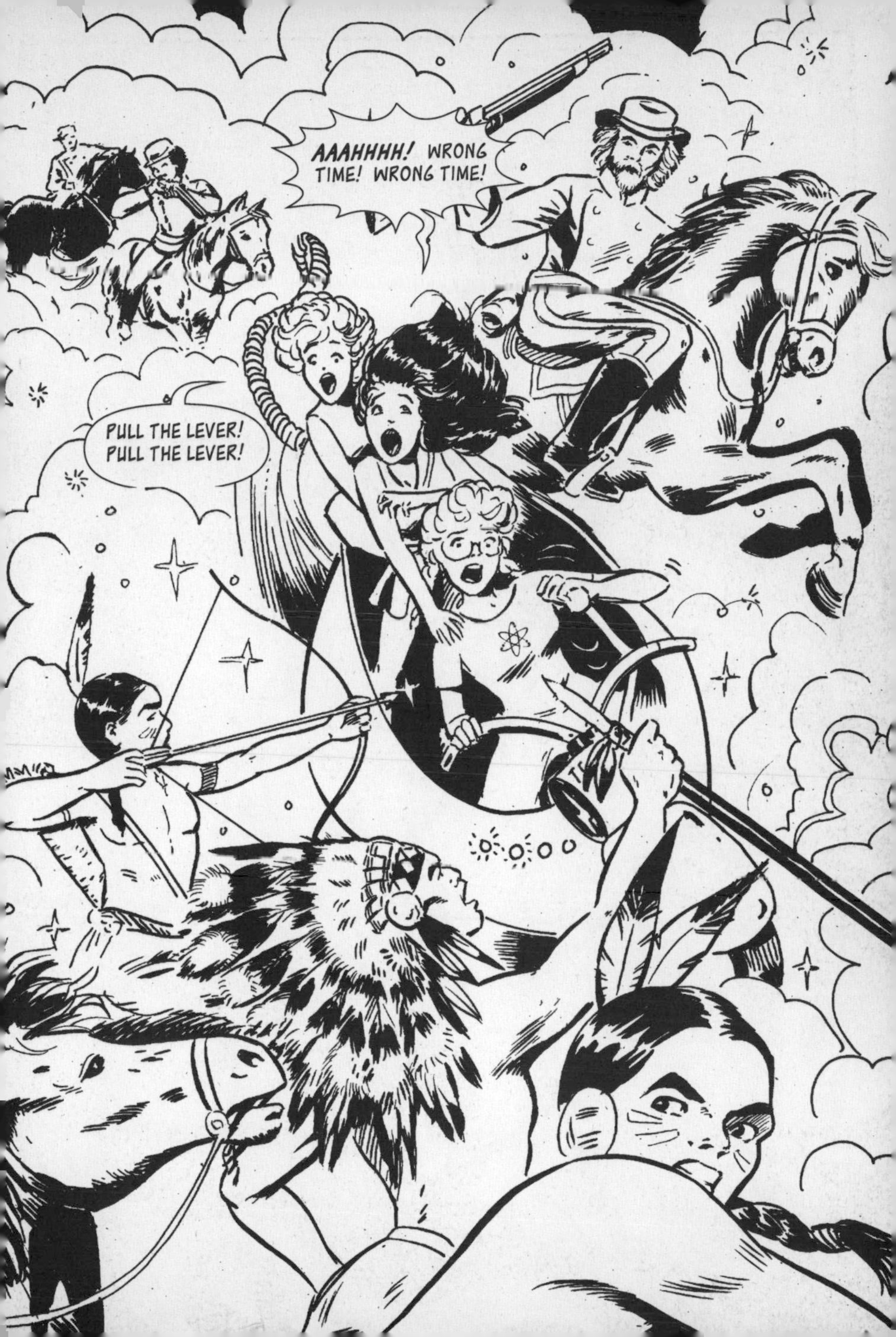
AAAHHHH! WRONG TIME! WRONG TIME!
PULL THE LEVER! PULL THE LEVER!

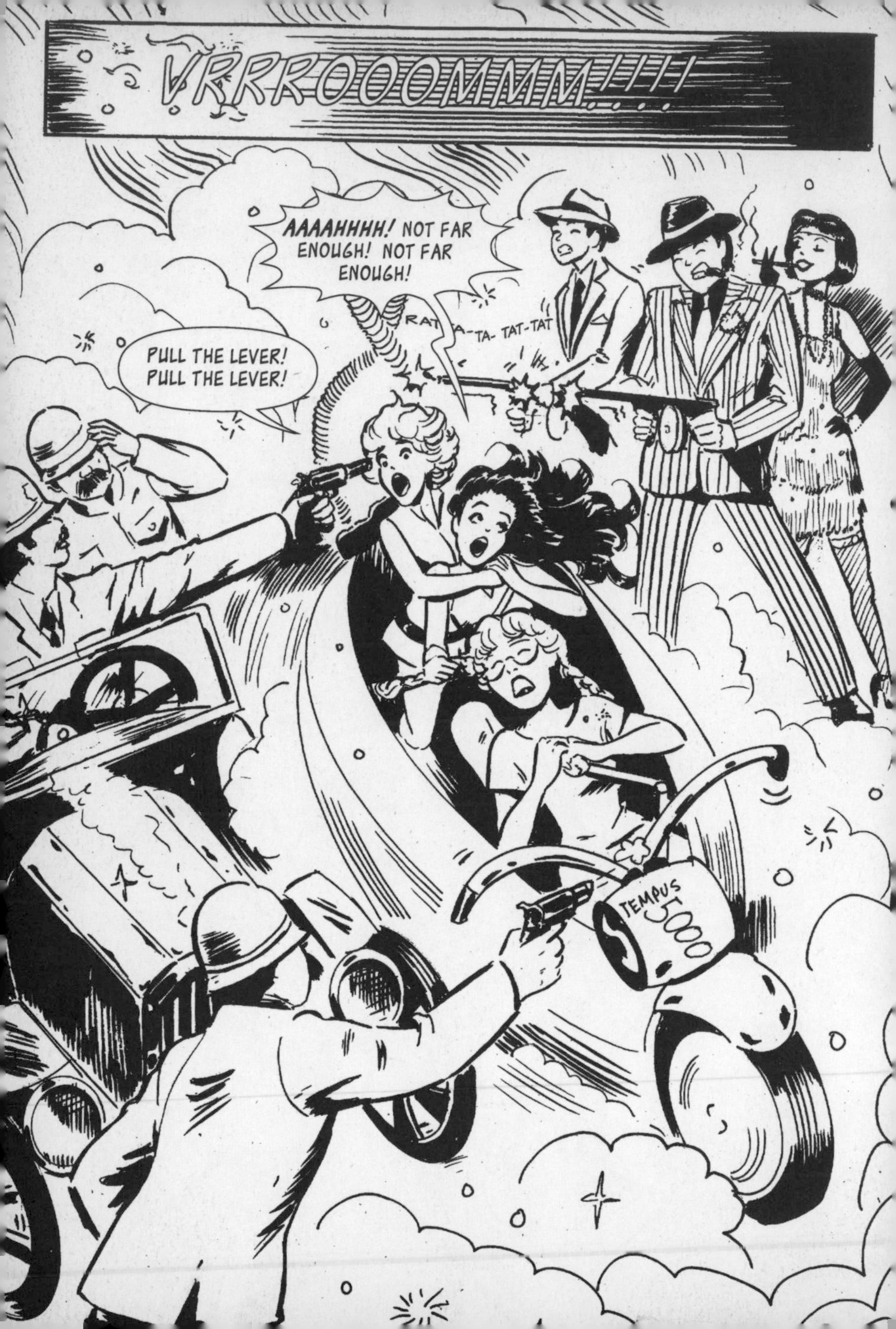
VRRROOOMMMM!!!!
AAAAHHHH! NOT FAR ENOUGH! NOT FAR ENOUGH!
PULL THE LEVER! PULL THE LEVER!
RAT-TA-TA-TAT-TAT
TEMPUS 5000

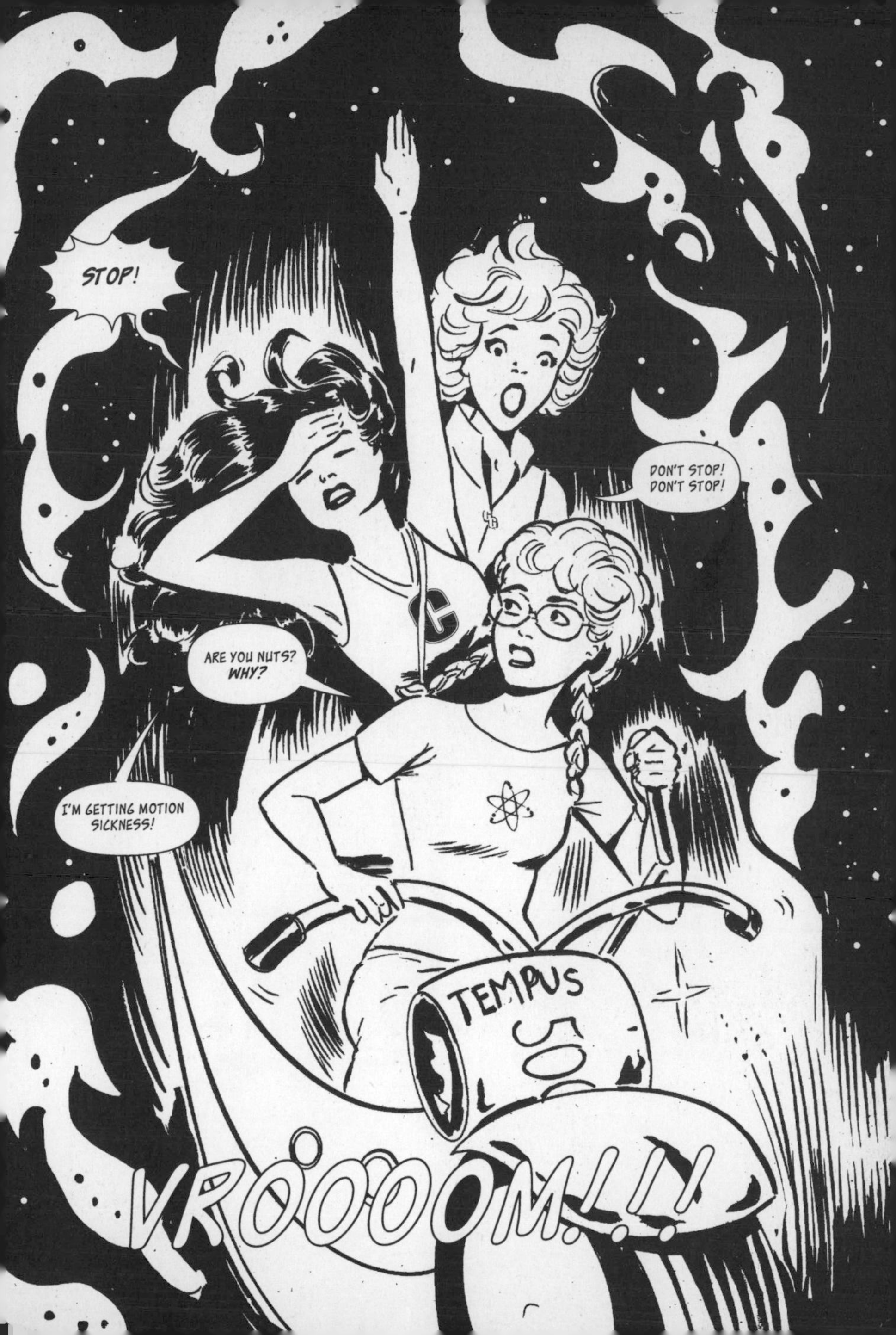
STOP!
DON'T STOP! DON'T STOP!
ARE YOU NUTS? WHY?
I'M GETTING MOTION SICKNESS!
TEMPUS
VROOOOOM!!!

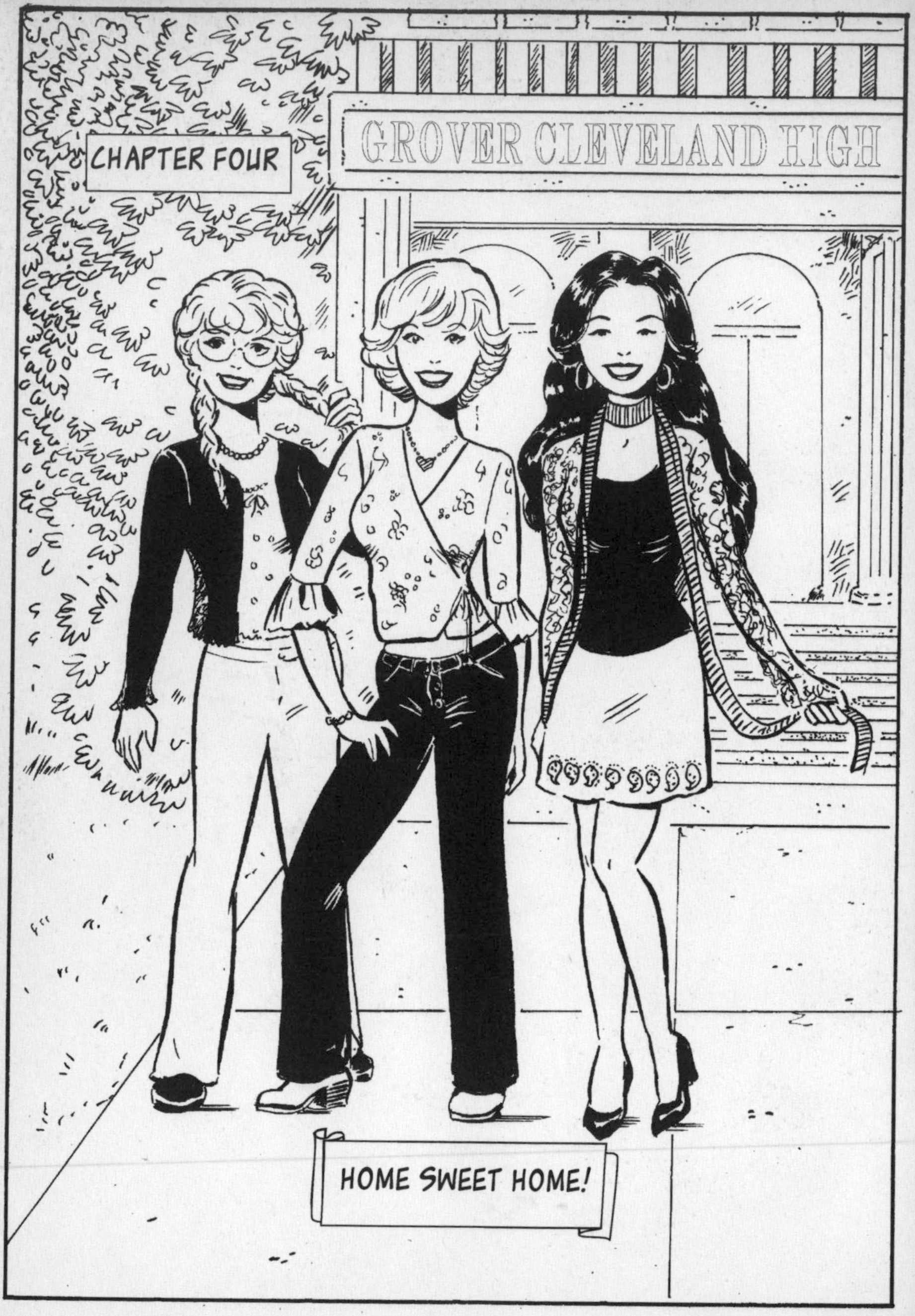
CHAPTER FOUR
GROVER CLEVELAND HIGH
HOME SWEET HOME!

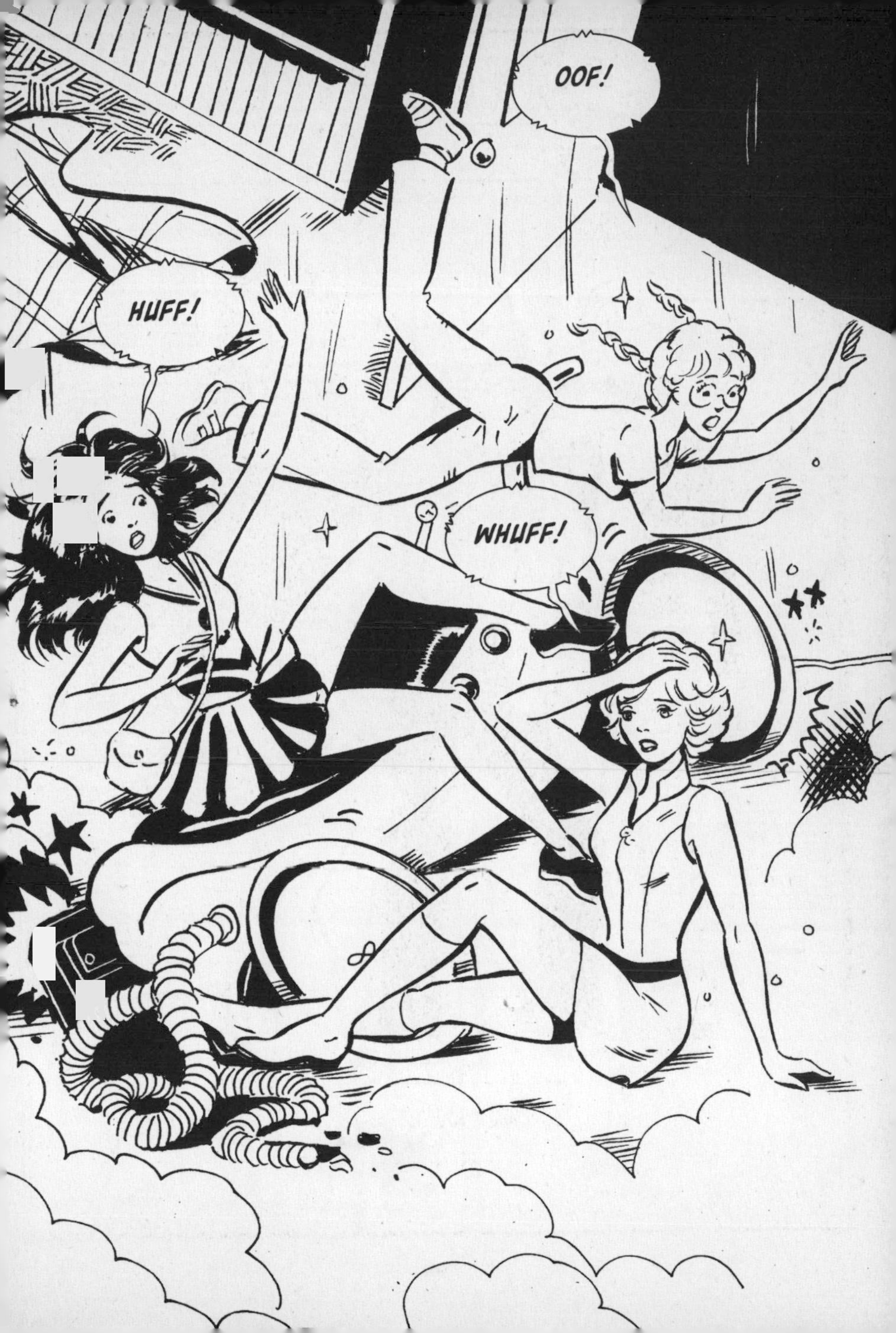
OOF!
HUFF!
WHUFF!

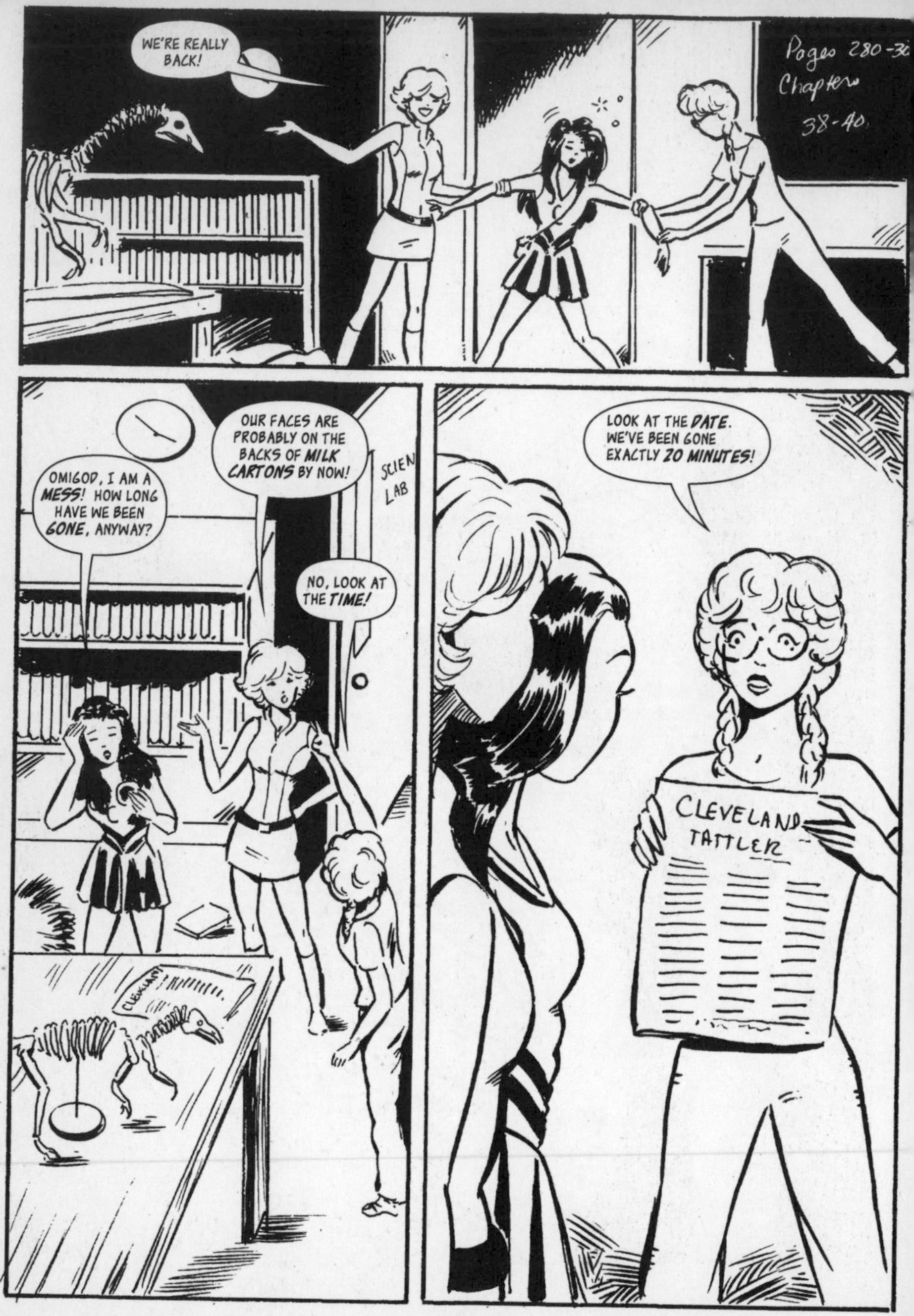
WE'RE REALLY BACK!
OMIGOD, I AM A MESS! HOW LONG HAVE WE BEEN GONE, ANYWAY?
OUR FACES ARE PROBABLY ON THE BACKS OF MILK CARTONS BY NOW!
SCIEN LAB
NO, LOOK AT THE TIME!
LOOK AT THE DATE. WE'VE BEEN GONE EXACTLY 20 MINUTES!
CLEVELAND TATTLER

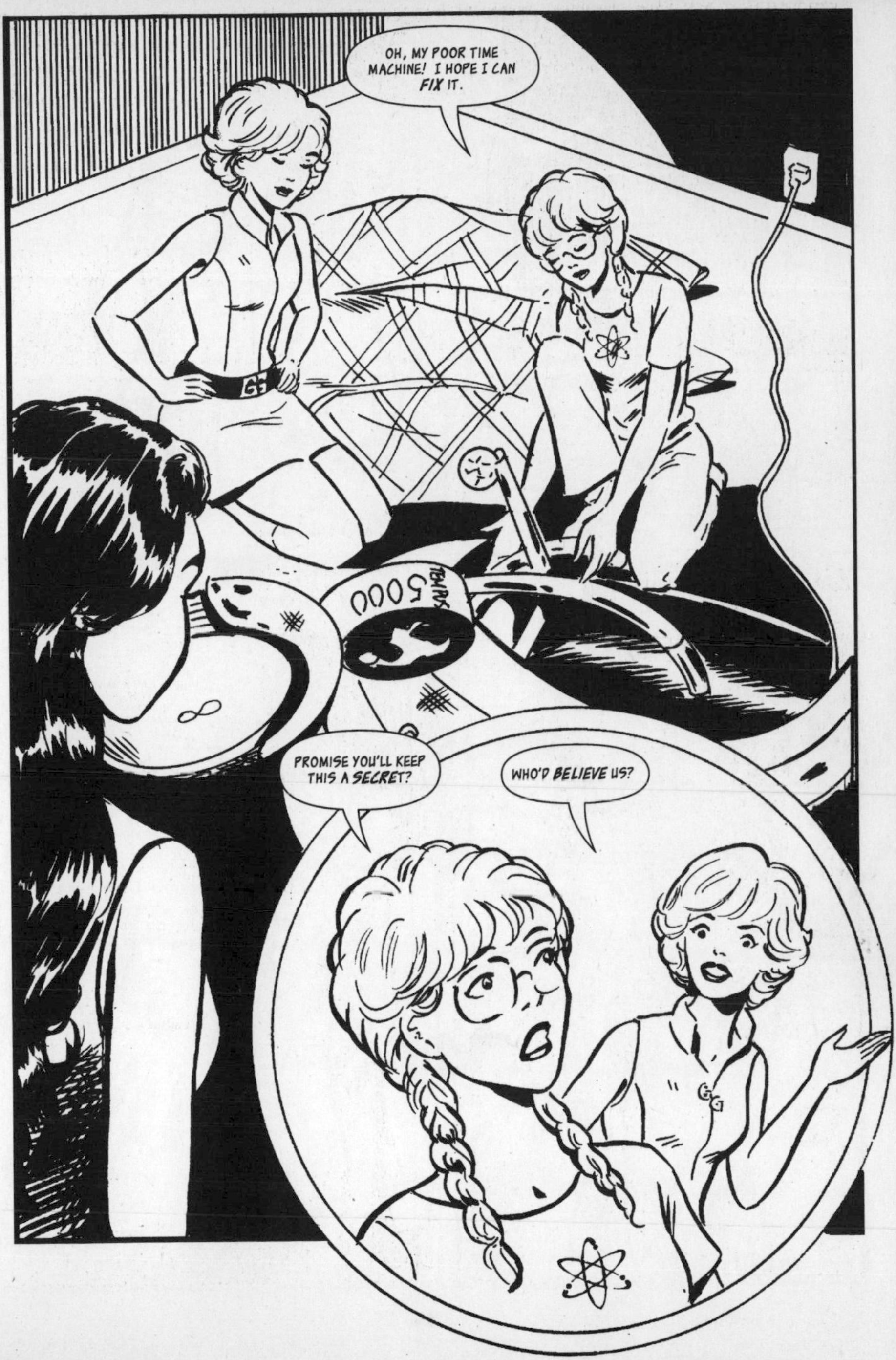
OH, MY POOR TIME MACHINE! I HOPE I CAN FIX IT.
5000
PROMISE YOU'LL KEEP THIS A SECRET?
WHO'D BELIEVE US?

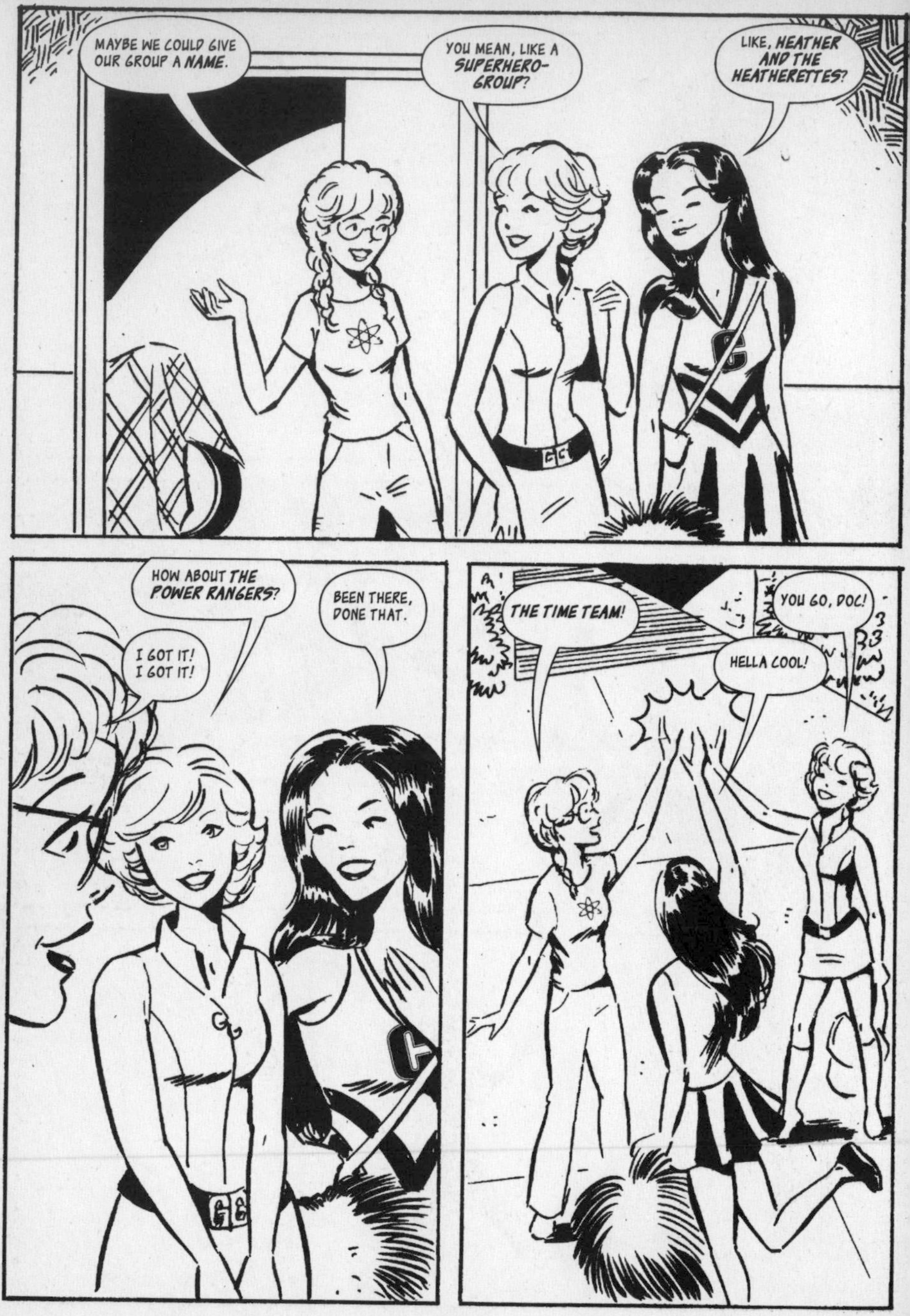
MAYBE WE COULD GIVE OUR GROUP A NAME.
YOU MEAN, LIKE A SUPERHERO-GROUP?
LIKE, HEATHER AND THE HEATHERETTES?
HOW ABOUT THE POWER RANGERS?
BEEN THERE, DONE THAT.
I GOT IT! I GOT IT!
THE TIME TEAM!
YOU GO, DOC!
HELLA COOL!

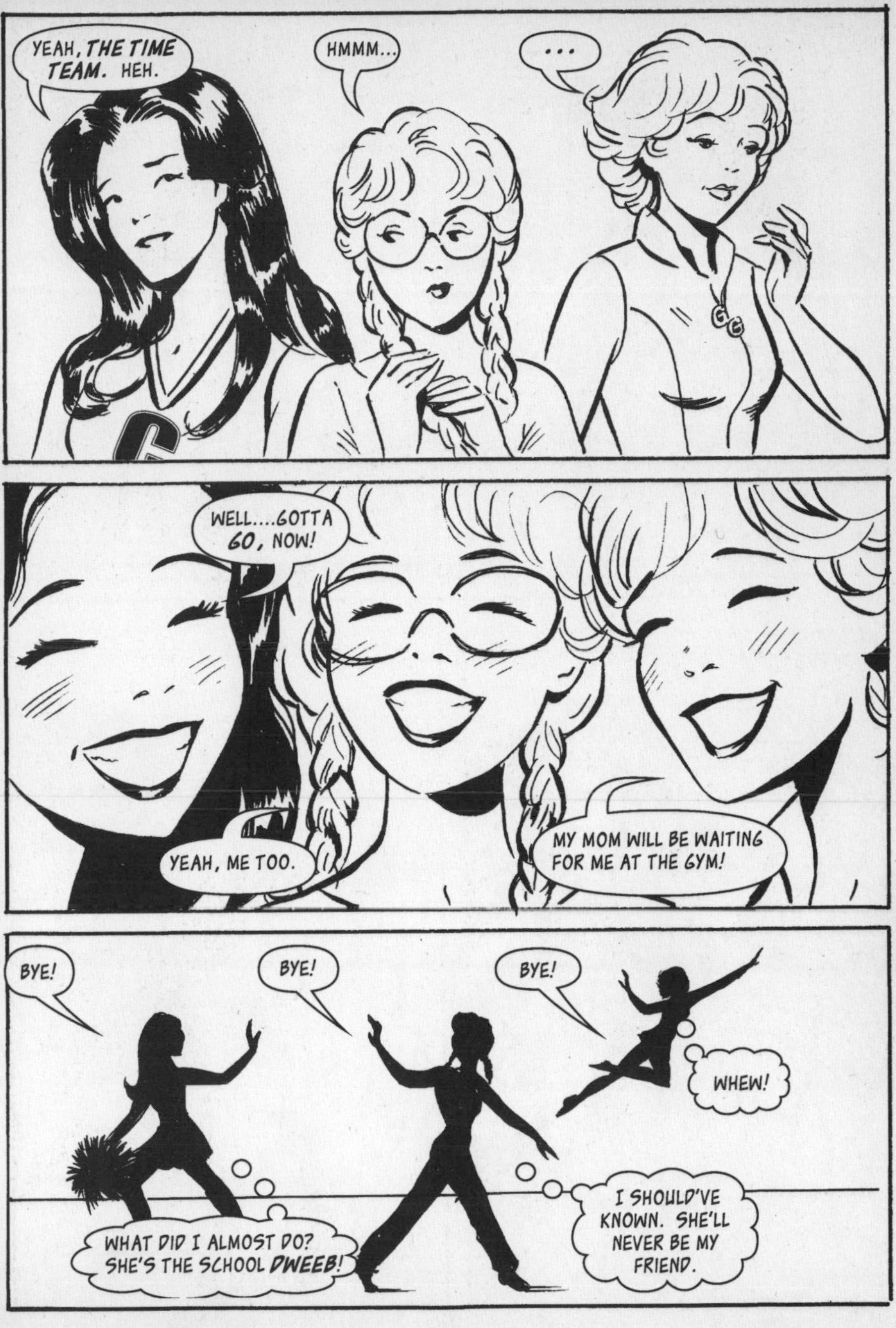
YEAH, *THE TIME TEAM*. HEH.
HMMM...
...
WELL....GOTTA *GO*, NOW!
YEAH, ME TOO.
MY MOM WILL BE WAITING FOR ME AT THE GYM!
BYE!
BYE!
BYE!
WHEW!
WHAT DID I ALMOST DO? SHE'S THE SCHOOL *DWEEB*!
I SHOULD'VE KNOWN. SHE'LL NEVER BE MY FRIEND.

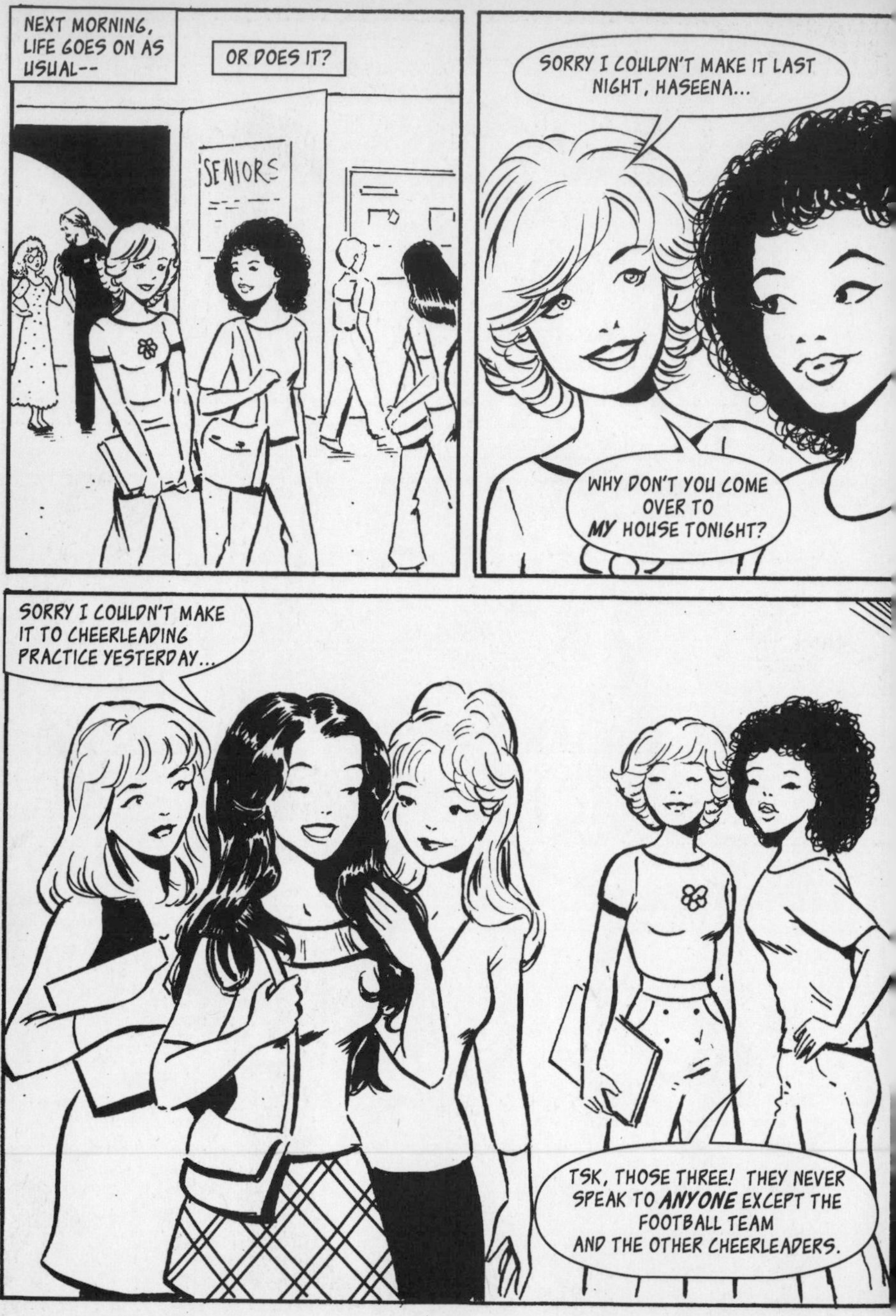
NEXT MORNING, LIFE GOES ON AS USUAL--
OR DOES IT?
SENIORS
SORRY I COULDN'T MAKE IT LAST NIGHT, HASEENA...
WHY DON'T YOU COME OVER TO *MY* HOUSE TONIGHT?
SORRY I COULDN'T MAKE IT TO CHEERLEADING PRACTICE YESTERDAY...
TSK, THOSE THREE! THEY NEVER SPEAK TO *ANYONE* EXCEPT THE FOOTBALL TEAM AND THE OTHER CHEERLEADERS.

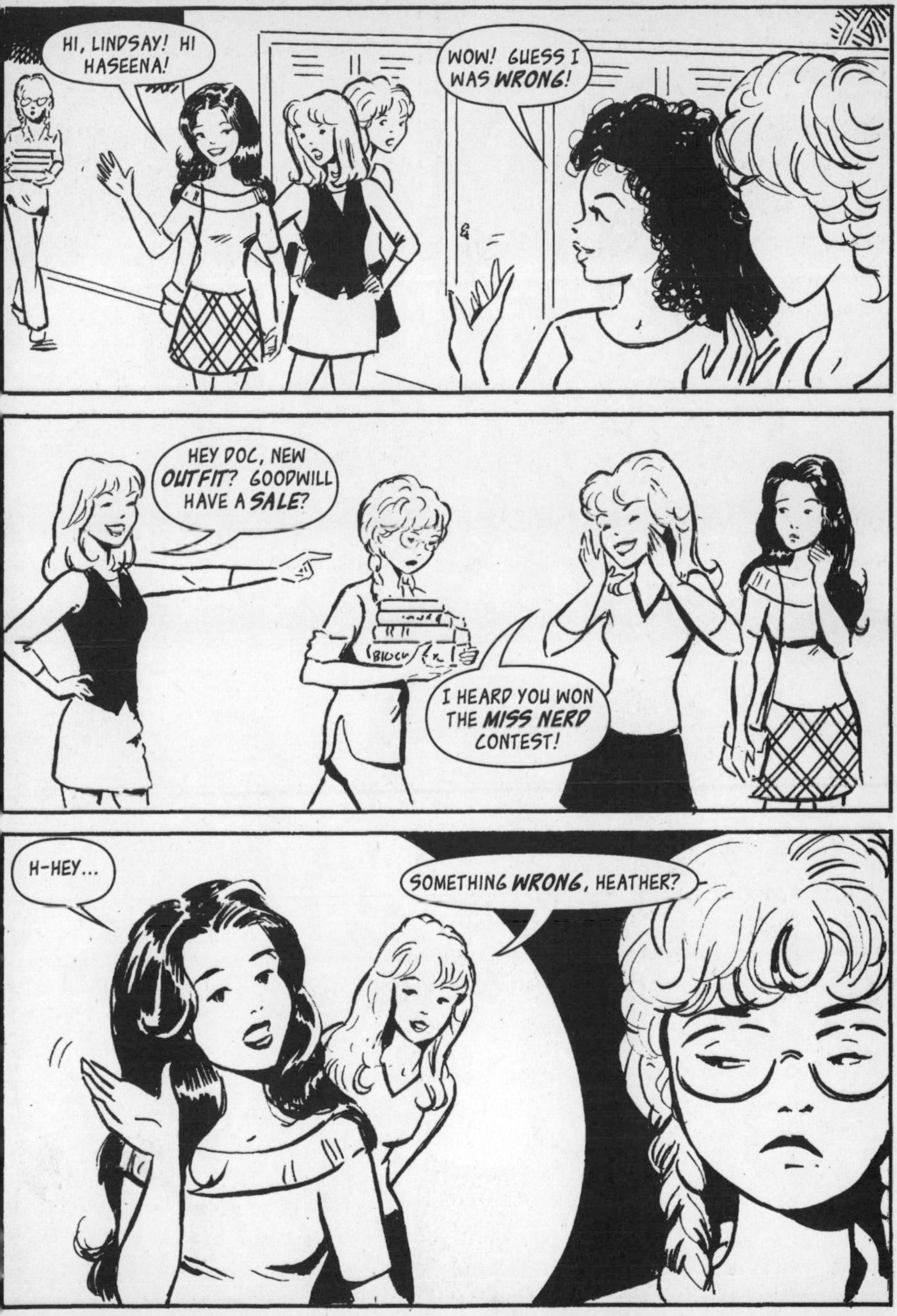
HI, LINDSAY! HI HASEENA!
WOW! GUESS I WAS WRONG!
HEY DOC, NEW OUTFIT? GOODWILL HAVE A SALE?
I HEARD YOU WON THE MISS NERD CONTEST!
H-HEY...
SOMETHING WRONG, HEATHER?

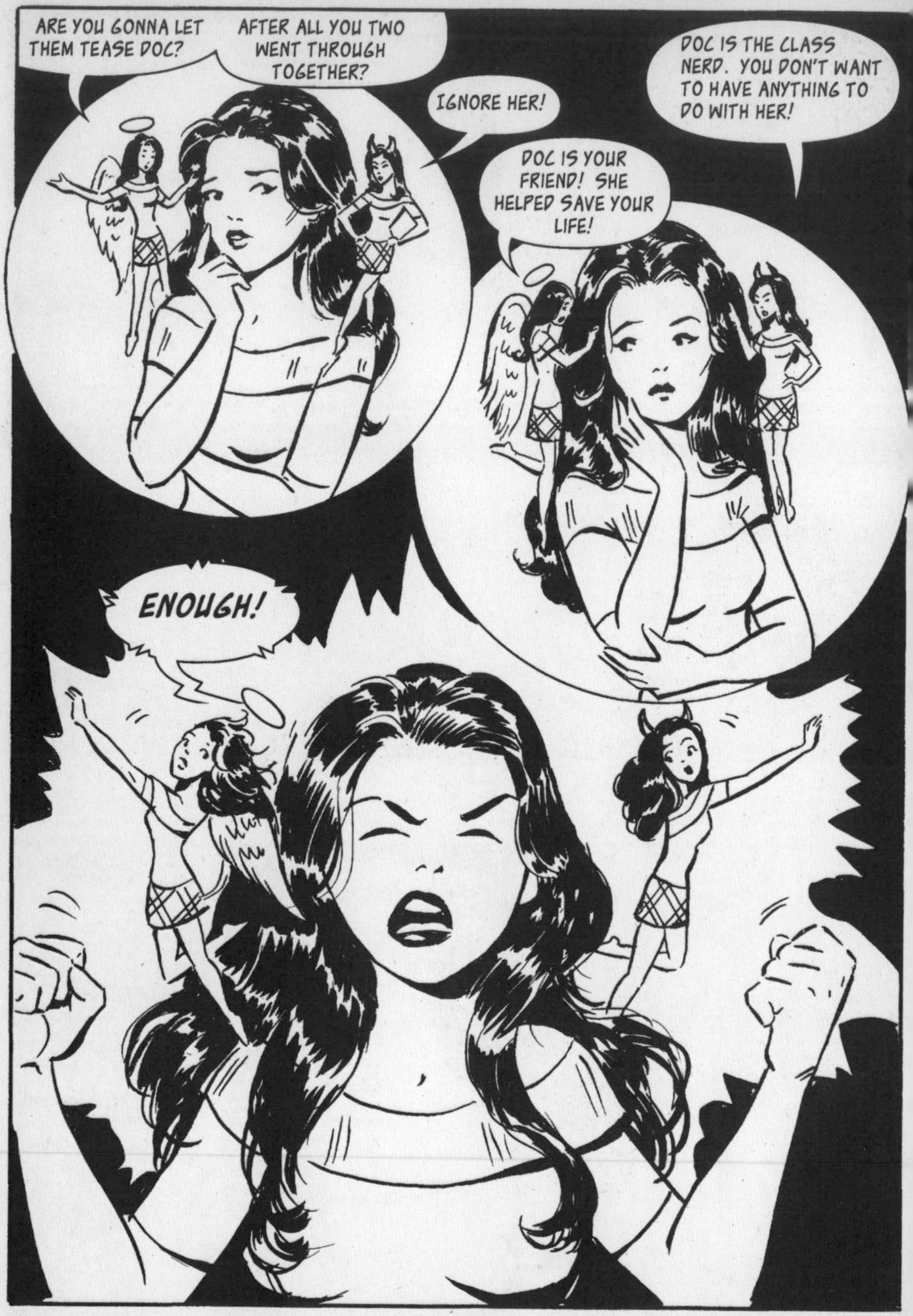
ARE YOU GONNA LET THEM TEASE DOC?
AFTER ALL YOU TWO WENT THROUGH TOGETHER?
IGNORE HER!
DOC IS THE CLASS NERD. YOU DON'T WANT TO HAVE ANYTHING TO DO WITH HER!
DOC IS YOUR FRIEND! SHE HELPED SAVE YOUR LIFE!
ENOUGH!

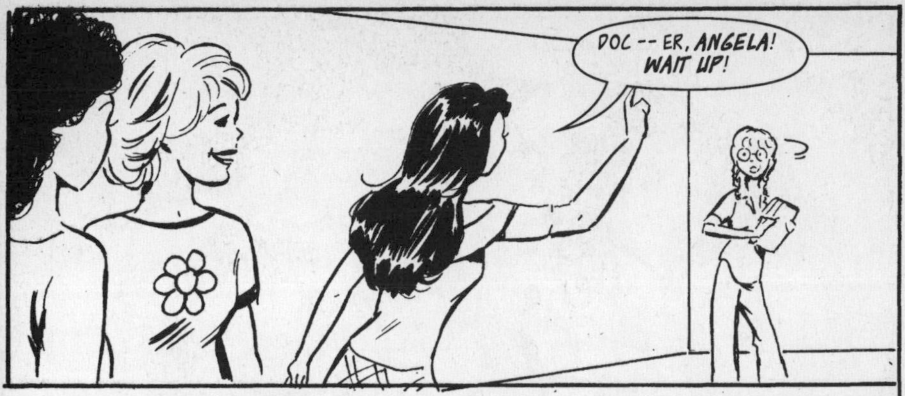
DOC -- ER, ANGELA! WAIT UP!

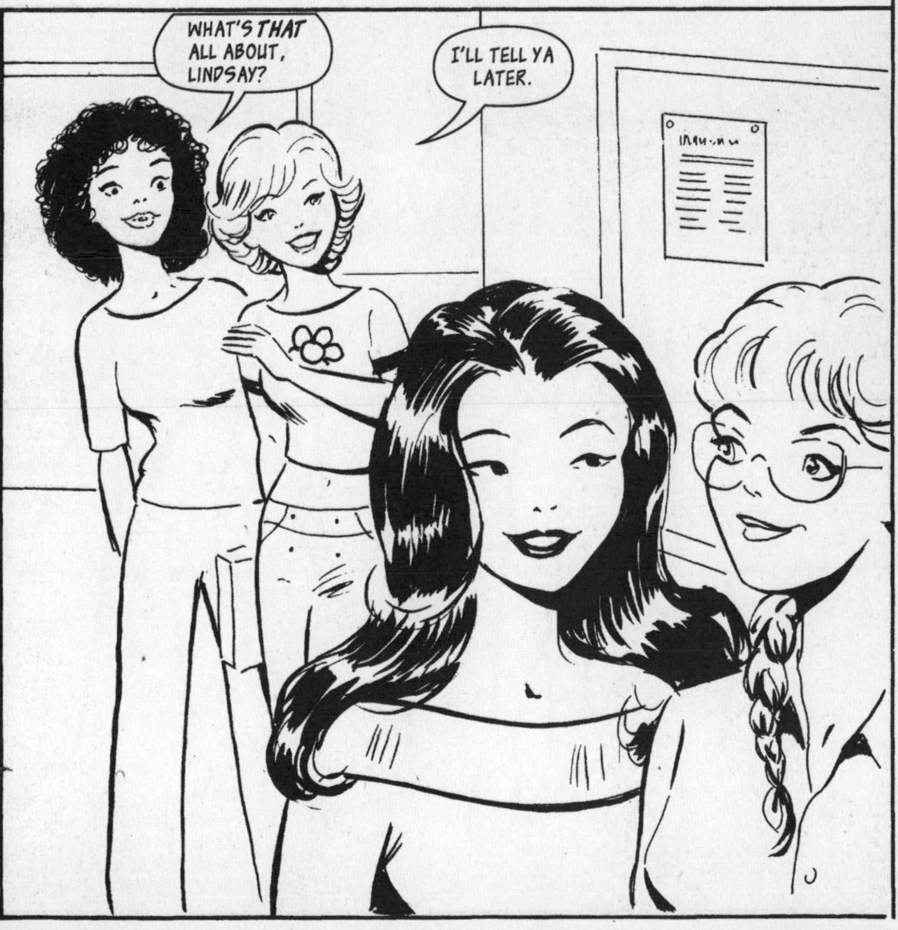
WHAT'S THAT ALL ABOUT, LINDSAY?
I'LL TELL YA LATER.

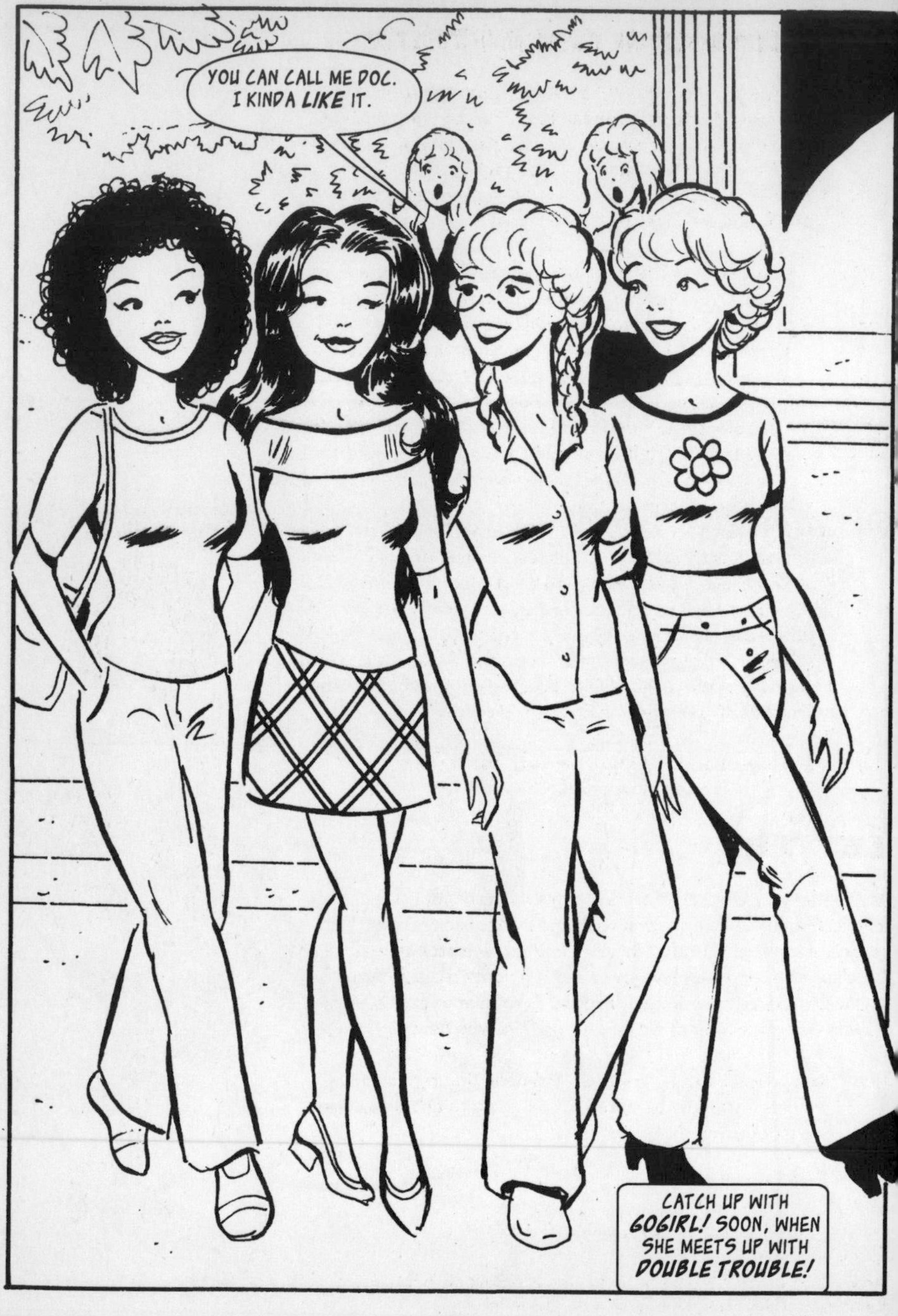

YOU CAN CALL ME DOC. I KINDA LIKE IT.
CATCH UP WITH GOGIRL! SOON, WHEN SHE MEETS UP WITH DOUBLE TROUBLE!

A WORD FROM THE AUTHOR

Hey everybody, we're back! WE are Anne Timmons, artist, and Trina Robbins (that's me!), creator and writer, and together we make up the team that gives you *GoGirl!* Last time you saw us was in Dark Horse's collection of the first five *GoGirl!* comics. Now we're back with *GoGirl!* coming to you regularly in a new format, and we hope you like her.

Because I know that we're not the only Go Girl in the world, I'm always on the lookout for other Go Girls, and this time I'd like to report on two great finds. One is a board game called *Go Goddess Girl!* It's all about empowerment, and players can find out which goddess they are from a list including Artemis, Athena, Isis, Venus, and Persephone. Best of all, there are beads to string into bracelets. The finished bracelets are supposed to read "Go Goddess Girl!" but we cheated and made bracelets that say "GoGirl!" You can find out more about this game on their website, www.gogoddessgirl.com.

Last year I found myself between planes for five (!) hours (can you believe it?) at Heathrow airport in England, so to kill some time I browsed the magazine rack, and guess what I found? A British magazine called *GoGirl!* There are no comics in it, but it's filled with full-color photos of movie and TV stars along with features like horoscopes, fashion tips, and photos and snippets from readers. If you're ever in England, pick up a copy!

If you find any other cool Go Girls, let us know!

—Trina Robbins

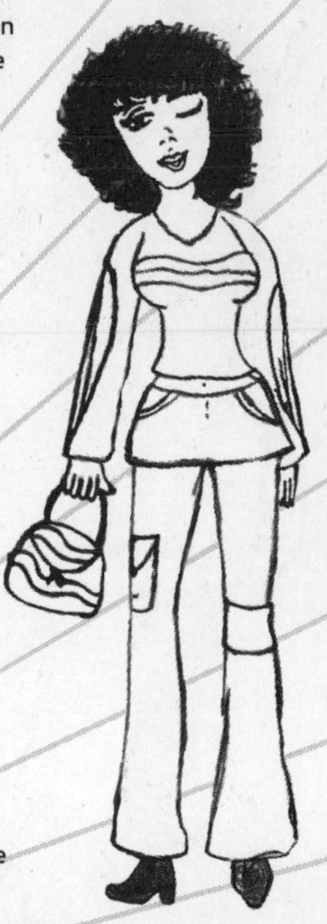

LETTERS

My twelve-year-old daughter and I are new fans of your *GoGirl!* comic. Found number one last weekend at a comic shop and simply adored it. My daughter and I both draw cartoons, and the superheroine mom/daughter act was right up our alley. I loved the reasons mom gave up flying. I too have an ex-husband who was kinda threatened by having a wife who flew.

Thank you so much for giving us someone that reflects us. I only had Supergirl before this. I am going to get your books and follow *GoGirl!*

Go, girl!
—Linda Place

You go, Linda, and keep flying!

Artwork on pages 95-96 sent in by Danielle Bullock, of Modesto, California, for Stylin' School Girl Lindsay and Hot Haseena. Thank you, Danielle!

Hi! My name's Amy! I live in a small city, and your comic makes living here a little more exciting. I've read it around eight times. It is based on an actual girl's life. Thats what I like about it. Well, hope you like my outfit.

—Amy Lawrence, Oil City, Pennsylvania

Thanks, Amy, and thanks for the cute jeans and top you sent for Lindsay to wear!

I've been meaning for a while now to take the time to write you. My boyfriend is a comics reader, and I like a few titles myself, but when I first saw the ad for *GoGirl!* in *Previews* a couple of years ago, I knew that the first issue would definitely be a comic that I HAD to buy.

The first issue finally came, and I wasn't disappointed. It reminded me so much of the comics that I liked when I was a little girl, combined with superheroes. I was instantly hooked. Finally! A comic by women, about women/girls, FOR women/girls. I bought the other four issues, as well. :)

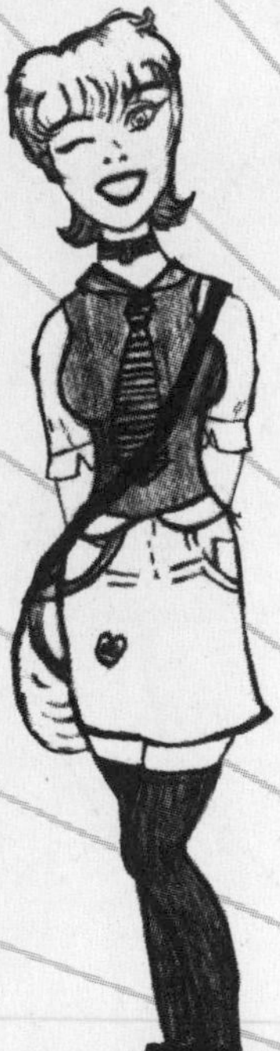

I was heartbroken when I thought that *GoGirl!* was over with issue 5. This was a comic that I would have LOVED just as much when I was girl if it had been around, and I could envision myself at that age even pretending to be GoGirl, along with She-Ra and Jem.

Then, I bought the trade paperback when it came out from Dark Horse Comics. But now...I have just learned that there is a NEW *GoGirl!* trade paperback coming out called *GoGirl!: The Time Team!!* (Of course, you know the name <smile>.) While I find it strange that it's "Volume 1", I couldn't be more excited. Ninety-six more pages of GoGirl! on September 8th!

Does this mean that there will be future TPs? If I had my way, there would be Volumes 2 through "Trina and Anne got tired of doing it." :)

I hope that the new book does well, and I've been promoting *GoGirl!* to all my friends since it came out. Now, even friends of mine who have never read comics have purchased their own copies of the original collection, and they're also excited about *The Time Team*. Because *GoGirl!* is my favorite comic book EVER, and Lindsay Goldman/GoGirl is my favorite superheroine (and I never thought that anyone would beat Supergirl for that position) of all time.

—Katherine Harland

Thank you, Katherine! And now you know that the new format GoGirl! *is indeed a continuing title, and so far Trina and Anne are NOT tired of doing it.*

LINDSAY'S WARDROBE

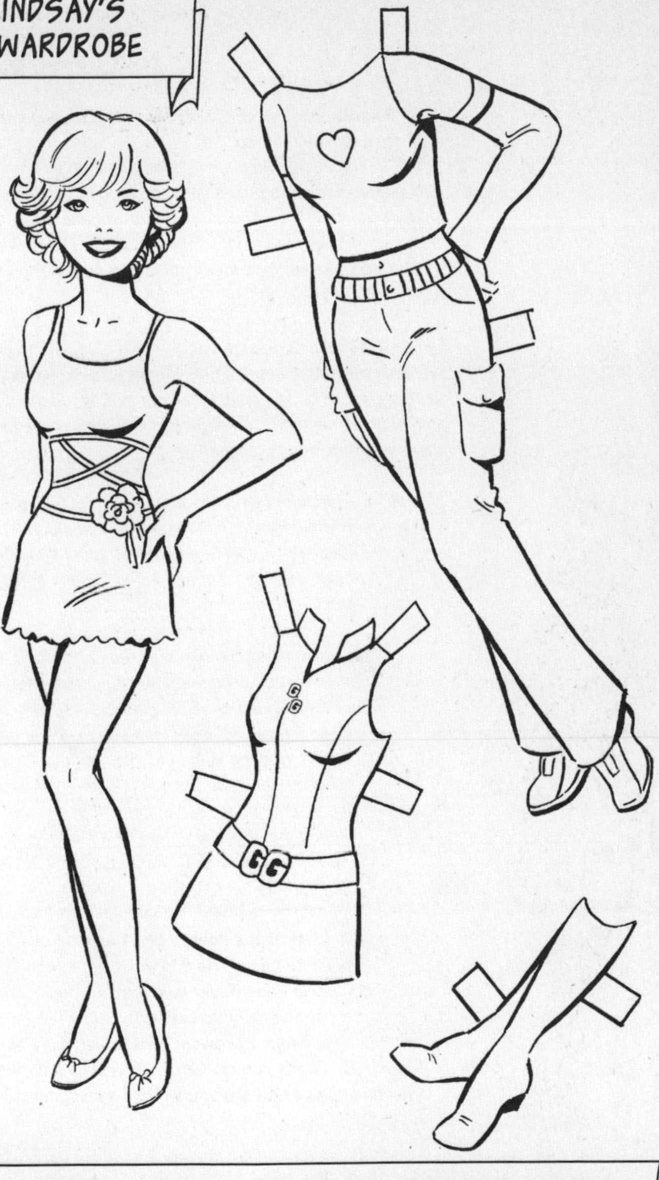

LINDSAY'S CUTE JEANS AND SHIRT WERE DESIGNED BY AMY LAWRENCE OF OIL CITY, PENNSYLVANIA.